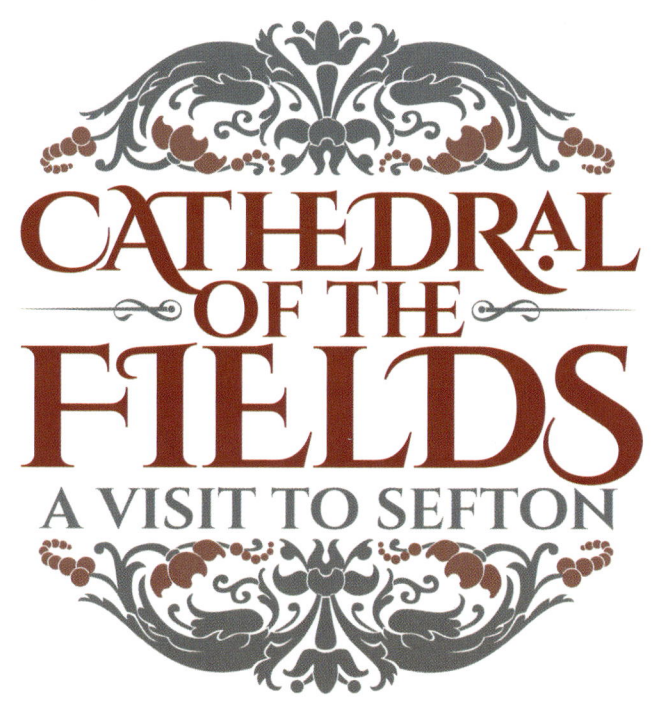

CATHEDRAL OF THE FIELDS

A VISIT TO SEFTON

GUIDE AND HISTORY OF
ST HELEN'S CHURCH, SEFTON

CW01497114

EDMUND J. CRIGHTON

Published in 2016
for The Friends of St Helen's Church, Sefton
by Mosslake Press
8 Gambier Terrace
Liverpool
L17BG

© Edmund J. Crighton 2016

All rights are reserved.
No part of this publication may be reproduced,
stored in a retrieval system, or transmitted in any form or by any means,
electronic, mechanical, photocopying or otherwise,
without the prior permission of both the copyright holder and the publisher.

The right of Edmund J. Crighton to be identified as the author
of this work has been asserted in accordance with the
Copyright, Designs and Patented Act 1988.

A CIP catalogue record for this book is available from the British Library.

ISBN 978-0-9955115-2-1 Guide
ISBN 978-0-9955115-0-7 Hardback
ISBN 978-0-9955115-1-4 Paperback

Cover: Skating at Sefton Meadows. Oil on canvas by M. Langton Knowles, October 1876.
Eighteenth-century oil on canvas of James Williamson, Recorder of Sefton, opposite page 115.

Design and production by Andrew Mather and AMA DataSet Limited, Preston.
Colour photography by Edmund J. Crighton and Robin Utracik.
Cover design, Church plan and Title page by Robin Utracik.

Printed and bound by Charlesworth Press, Wakefield WF2 9LP

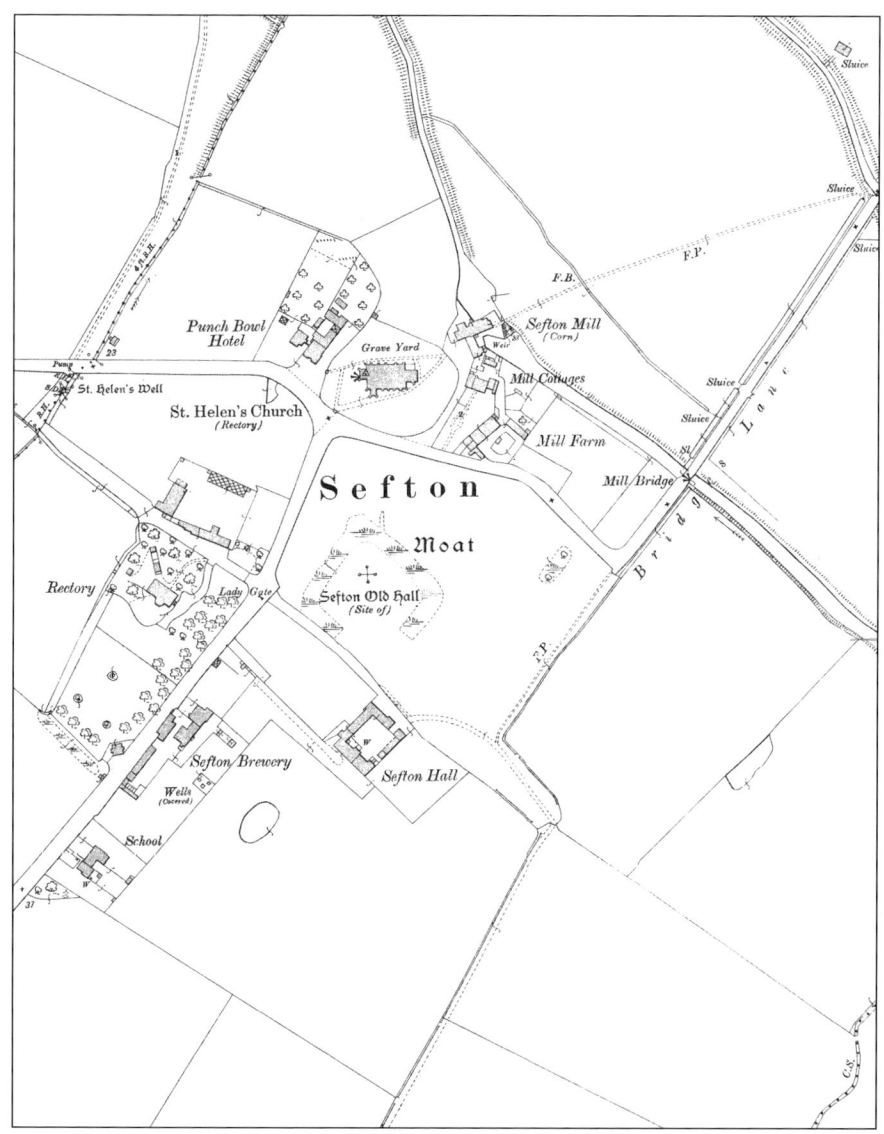

This book is dedicated to St Helena (*c.* 249–329),
mother of Constantine the Great.

We adore Thee, O Christ, and we praise Thee,
because by Thy Holy Cross Thou hast redeemed the world.

St Francis of Assisi

SPONSORS

MARK BLUNDELL　　CHRISTOPHER RAINSHAW ROTHWELL

TERRY AND JANE CAVE

STEPHEN GUY

DILLY AND MAURICE HAYMAN

HELEN HUNTER

WILLIAM DARGUE TYRER KIDD

CANON TIMOTHY LIPSCOMB

ANDREW MATHER

HILARY AND ALAN MCMULLIN

MERCHANT TAYLORS' SCHOOLS CROSBY

GINA PORTER

PATRICK J POWER

JOHN AND FRANCES QUIRK

EDWARD W. ROBERTS

J. PETER AND JEANETTE ROTHWELL

KEITH AND SYBIL THOMAS

FOREWORD

For years, Edmund Crighton has been fascinated by the history of the parish of Sefton. He has now written not only a guide book but this substantial volume. My family has had a long connection with Sefton Church, and I am honoured that he has asked me to write a Foreword.

St Helen's Church is one of the most historic buildings of Lancashire. Dating back to the twelfth century, it was first built by members of the Molyneux family who much later became Earls of Sefton. In those days, they were the first family of Lancashire. Two lesser local families were also involved at an early stage, the Blundells of Ince, who later acquired many valuable estates and a famous art collection, and the almost unrelated Blundells of Little Crosby. With St Helen's Church nearby, the three families lived side by side for seven centuries or so. Generally, but not always, their relations were harmonious.

The Manor of Little Crosby has been held by the Blundells since 1362, when they unexpectedly acquired it through a marriage to a Molyneux daughter, with the help of the Black Death which had killed off rival claimants. The Molyneux of the time were not impressed with this turn of events and there was a vicious territorial challenge in the early sixteenth century, led by Edward Molyneux, Rector of Sefton. Both families prayed at St Helen's Church – but not hard enough, it appears. After the Reformation, for two hundred years all three families remained (mainly) Roman Catholic. Like all medieval churches, St Helen's became Anglican. This was, to say the least, an awkward situation for the Rectors of Sefton. The religious persecutions of the sixteenth and seventeenth centuries are notorious and there were many opportunities for conflict. Rector Nutter was (probably) responsible for the arrest of Richard and William Blundell in 1590 which was followed by their imprisonment in Lancaster Castle. It was Rector Turner's refusal to allow Catholics to be buried in Sefton churchyard that lead to the creation of the Harkirk burial ground at Crosby Hall in 1611.

Gradually, over the centuries, the religious conflicts died down. A century later Nicholas Blundell was appointed a churchwarden – admittedly, against his will. In time, differences of Christian faith became more acceptable and today there is an abundance of goodwill among all those interested in the long history of Sefton.

Edmund Crighton's book is the first for many decades to get to grips with the history of St Helen's Church. It includes much fascinating material – the Mock Corporation of Sefton, to take one example, is a charming piece of social history (though it is hard to believe that Patrick Cotter was indeed 8ft 7ins tall!). The book deserves a wide and appreciative readership.

Mark Blundell
Little Crosby
September 2016

WELCOME

For centuries, Sefton Church has dominated the flat sandy soil of south west Lancashire as it slips imperceptibly towards the sea. In a landscape devoid of great abbeys and churches, it is hardly surprising that Sefton was often called *The Cathedral of the Fields.*

Sefton Church has grown organically over more than eight hundred years, and what was once shockingly modern is now weather-beaten, and warm. On its worn stones, knights in armour have knelt and prayed long nights before battles in distant theatres of war, and controversy has raged within its confines, dividing and uniting all. Today, it remains a living testament to the past and a shining beacon of a living and joyous Christian faith – one which we can all share and celebrate.

This is the story of Sefton and its Church.

The Stones Speak

We do not know which came first – the manor house or church [1]. It is most probable that the Molyneux family, who arrived after 1066, built their manor house before raising a small chapel nearby. In Dod's MS, vol, lxi, we find the following:

> *Guilliam Desmolines is ye 18th man in ye catalogue or Rowle of the Noblemen which came with the Conqueror, and likewise made mention of in ye Chronicle of Odo Bishoppe of Bayeu, wheare he rehearseth ye names of ye men of accompte remayninge or live after ye 1st Battaile fought agt. Kinge Harold in Sussex 1067. At Sephton this G.M. builded his chiefe house at ye which from yt time to this day his heirs mascles have continually kepte their chiefe aboade in estate of knight for ye most part of them.*

The manor house has now disappeared almost without trace, but the church, most certainly embellished by the family, fortunately has survived.

It is difficult to establish the date of the church's foundation but we have several clues. When viewed from the air, the site's distinct oval outline can clearly be seen, which is a feature of Saxon cemeteries. Possibly a cemetery predated the church building. Fragments of stone carvings [2] found during various restorations suggest a date of about 1170 – the same as Ormskirk Church. We have some documentary evidence, but other written material may have perished or may still be undiscovered. The earliest extant document concerns a dispute between the prior and monks of Lancaster Priory and Richard (Parson of Sefton) and Robert of Walton, his vicar, about two sheaves of tithe. Although undated, luckily it mentions being written in the sixth year of Pope Innocent III – which puts it at 1204/5.[1] The next document to mention Sefton is in the Valour of Pope Nicholas, and dated 1291, which concerns taxation for Edward I's Crusades to the Holy Land: 'Ecclia de Cefton ... £26 : 13 : 4. (Sp. Decima) ... £2 : 13 : 4.' From this document we know that Sefton was in the Deanery of Warrington and the Diocese of Coventry at the time.

We must make up our own minds on this evidence.

A distraction to the dating of the building is the carving over the porch door, which appears to declare the date AD IIII. This is, in fact, a weathered monogram and nothing to do with the date. The porch was restored in 1919 by Johan Frederik Caröe (brother of W. D. Caröe) in memory of his wife Eleanor.

[3]

It is thought that the earliest chapel stood where the present Chancel stands today. By the fifteenth century there was an aisleless church with the current steeple and the Lady Chapel attached to the north side. In the late fifteenth century, it was decided to enlarge the church considerably by building a new Chancel and a nave with north and south aisles. It is probable that this work was nearing completion in the 1530s as the two chantries – one in each aisle, were founded in 1528 and 1535. The Margaret Bulcley window was placed in the centre light of the south aisle about 1543, by which time other new windows were already in place.

The 'new' rood screen [3] must have been carved by the same craftsman who worked for the Ireland Family at nearby Lydiate Hall. Some of the lower panels of the Sefton screen, which sadly have been replaced, used to be an exact match for those at Lydiate. After Lydiate, which was dated 1514, the carver's next job was probably at Sefton. There is also a similar carving at Towneley Hall, near Burnley, on panels which used to be in the pre-Reformation Chapel, maybe as part of the original rood screen.

[4]

All the evidence seems to imply that the church was rebuilt by a succession of Molyneux priests: James (1489–1509), Edward (1509–1535) and ending with Anthony [4] (1535–1557). Anthony Molyneux may have been given the task of completing it – particularly the Chancel, where he wished to be buried (if he died at Sefton). He mentions the Chancel, revestry and parsonage [5] in his Will, but not the nave.

Written in Stone – how the building grew

We may never know exactly how the building grew but what follows is a possible scenario.

[5]

SEFTON   DURHAM

[6]

First known building – 1170

As our mediaeval builders did not leave behind their plans, their records are written in stone. Pieces of masonry unearthed during the replacement of the east window in the nineteenth century suggest that the earliest known building was built in the Transitional Norman style as they match exactly those in the narthex of Durham Cathedral [6] which are dated 1170. It was likely to have been a modest building whose fragments may be seen today in the south-east chapel by the Molyneux tombs.

[7]

Lady Chapel – 1300

A small, square Lady Chapel [7] was added to the north east of this church about 1300. This makes the north-east corner one of the oldest parts of the current building.

Nave and north aisle – 1320

About 20 years later around 1320 the church was dramatically enlarged by building a new nave, north aisle and steeple, while the old church was reordered into a Chancel – all in the Early English style.

Lady Chapel extended – 1415

In the early fifteenth century, around 1415, the Lady Chapel was extended westwards and the north aisle extended north and raised to join up with the Lady Chapel.

New Nave and Chancel – 1500

[8]

During the Incumbency of Archdeacon James Molyneux, around 1500, this piecemeal building, save for the Lady Chapel and steeple, was torn down and replaced with a much grander building, in the airy Perpendicular style [8]. Many earlier historians have ascribed this work to Anthony Molyneux, who was Priest from 1535–1557, but documentary evidence does not bear this out. Dodsworth, a fairly reliable north country antiquarian, mentions that Anthony built the schoolhouse at Sefton, yet he does not mention the church. Anthony, in his own Will, mentions that he cannot be charged for *dylapidations for Sefton as at ye chauncell and revestre and at ye psonage after making so great coste there.*[2] As Rector he was legally responsible for the Chancel and parsonage.

[9]

The new building [9] was attached to the old steeple, and consisted of nave, Lady Chapel, porch, revestry, Chancel and two aisles. The Chancel may have been completed by Anthony.

There is a suspicion that the old steeple was originally doomed as careful examination of its abutment to the new nave reveals that it does not line up properly as one would expect. The new nave is a fraction to the south of the old one and it looks like a hasty decision has been made to join the two together.[3] Maybe a new steeple was abandoned because of the growing instability in the country on account of war with the Scots and the icy winds of the Reformation being felt at Sefton.

Those with an interest in archaeology will find evidence of building stages by examining the stonework in the Lady Chapel, the north-east internal wall and the remains of a window and stone-work abutments where the tower meets the north-west wall. Look high up above the west wall arch and you will find the original steep roof line of about 1320.

In 1915 a choir vestry was added and in the late twentieth century, a small kitchen and lavatory. Electricity was only introduced in 1971.

A pleasant spot

Ceffton, Sextone, Sephton or Sefton?

While spelling was only standardised in the sixteenth century, the name of the village has varied even into the twentieth century. In the Doomsday Survey of 1089, it is called 'Sextone' and owned by Roger de Poitou who was also known as Roger of **Pictavencis, or in the West Riding as Roger le Poitevin. Recently, an 8,000-year-old human settlement has been found at Lunt Meadows down by the river. Annoyingly, the name of Liverpool does not appear in Doomsday and is not mentioned in an extant document until 1191 although its famous Calderstones date back about 3000 years. The isolated fishing village of Liverpool was in the parish of Walton until 1699, and its church, which was probably a Minster, still retains its Saxon font.**

Thomas Pennant (1726–1798), the Welsh naturalist, traveller, writer and antiquarian described Sefton in 1773 as 'placed on a vast range of fine meadows, that reach almost to the sea and in a great measure supply Liverpool with hay' [10].

Until the middle of the twentieth century, the River Alt was rich in trout and ran very close to the church. In winter, the meadows flooded and in freezing weather provided skating facilities for people from far and wide. It is known that actors and actresses from the Liverpool theatres came here on the train to Sefton and Maghull Station for refreshment. Jane Mason 1883–1965 (née Molyneux, but pronounced Molinex) ran a tea shop in her front room of Mill Cottage for visitors to the church and meadows. Many of her customers kept in touch throughout the year. The church owns a late nineteenth-century painting of 'Skating on Sefton Meadows'. We also have a drawing of another similar scene from the early nineteenth century.

[10]

9

[11]

On the site of the Manor House, immediately south of the church, there was a spring and well which provided fresh water. To the west is the sandy coast and to the north there used to be the vast lake of Martin Mere (now greatly reduced in size).

THE TOUR

Our tour of the church is divided into 20 stations – places to pause and reflect. We start our journey outside the porch.

1

As you approach the porch [11], built about 1500, look up and see the worn shield with what appears to be IhC inscribed upon it. Higher still above the window is a niche, now holding a statue. Before the Reformation this probably held a statue of the Virgin Mary, but now holds a representation of St Helen, to whom the church is dedicated. Inside, notice the original oak doors with their sixteenth-century hinges. Through the door and on the left there is an Alms' box, designed by W. D. Caröe FSA (1913) and placed in memory of Eleanor Jane Alexander Caröe (his sister-in-law 1863–1913). Above the porch is a small room, the Parvise (not open to the public). It might have been used by the Chantry priest as a vestry or living quarters.

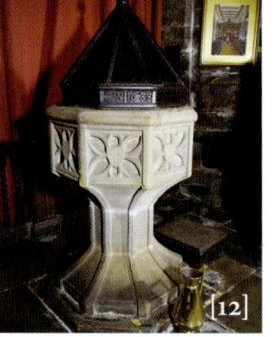
[12]

2

Standing at the back of the church, we can enjoy a panoramic view of the inside of the building. Behind us the red sandstone font [12] (late fourteenth-century) is octagonal, with blank shields in six-foils on each face and raised fillets on the angles of bowl, stem and base. Repairs to the lip suggest an earlier lockable lid. Its present pyramidal 'candle-snuffer' oak cover, which is inscribed 'R R : H M : C W. 1688', was originally painted in white, vermillion and gold. The font was also originally painted in bright colours: at the Reformation it was whitewashed; now it is bare stone. Until the early twentieth century it stood underneath the tower.

[13]

Ringing Chamber

Behind the font is the Ringing Chamber under the tower.

Above the low door to the tower staircase is a stone tablet commemorating the restoration of the tower in 1843 by Mary Birchall and Richard Rainshaw Rothwell, dedicated to the Glory of God and in memory of Sarah Rothwell.

In all three walls there is a rectangular recess, one of which may have been used to store the chrismatory containing the Holy Oils.

There is a suspicion that this area could have been the priest's vestry and these lockers used for storage.

On the wall are some ringing memorials, including two modern ones of English oak [13], made to complement other carvings around the church.

Note the fine window in the tower [14], with masonry of the late fifteenth century. The tracery is very similar to the fine piscina which we shall see in the Mollinex Chantry (Station 10).

The Clock

Although the faces can be read from outside (and one face above the interior west arch), the workings [15 and 16] are above the ringing chamber and not accessible to the public. Made by Smith of Derby, it was a gift from Richard Rainshaw Rothwell Esq of Sefton (1904) and replaced an earlier one which had been installed in 1818 at a cost of £167.

The Bells

Bells are inextricably linked to the worshiping life of the Church. Tower bells call the faithful to services and in earlier times would have rung out the Angelus at 6.00am, 12 noon and 6.00pm. Inside church, smaller bells (sacring bells) would ring at the elevation of the host during the Mass.

Unfortunately the bells [17] cannot be seen as they are high in the tower, out of sight. Please do NOT touch the bell ropes as they can be dangerous.

Although the oldest bells date from about 1588, we do know that the church had even earlier bells. The 1552 Inventory lists 'Four bells, Two sacring bells'.

The present tower bells form an octave, cast in four pairs of bells dating from different periods.

Two older and two new bells were placed in a new oak frame in 1601 while two more were added in 1815. It is noted in the Church-wardens' accounts on 17th March 1815 that at a Vestry meeting, it was ordered that: 'two new additional bells shall be hung in the steeple, and that Mr. Dobson of Downham-Market furnish the same'. Later in the same year, we find, 'Paid Mr. Dobson for the bells £199 11s. 4d'.

The ring of six bells was opened on the 26th December 1815, and the expenses for that event amounted to a staggering £16 16s 10d. A Mr Fisher was paid £5 for 'engraveing' and examining the bells, and William Parr, a builder, was paid £39 12s, 'as by bill'. It is interesting to note that the massive oak beams which were added in 1815 had evidently been used before elsewhere and there is a well-founded suspicion that they came from Sefton Hall which was being

dismantled at that time. All this oak was removed at the end of the Second World War when a new steel frame [18] for eight bells was installed.

7 and 8 are the heaviest and oldest pair of bells and might have been cast in thanksgiving for the delivery from the Spanish Armada in 1588.

5 and 6 are dated 1601 and might have marked the new century (new centuries begin with 01, not 00).

3 and 4 are dated 1815 and no doubt celebrate the victory at Waterloo on 18th June 1815.

1 and 2 memorialise the Victory in the Second World War in 1945.

Although of different periods, they sound remarkably well together and form a scale in the key of F. Number 1 is the lightest bell with the highest note (treble), with 8 being the heaviest (tenor) and deepest note. At a height of 50 feet, they are rung from the ground floor and the tenor weighs 11 cwt. 2 qrts. 11 lbs. (589 kg).

The Dog-Whippers' Pew

Flanking the Font to the south is the Dog-Whippers' Pew. The Dog-Whipper [19] here shown at St Bavo's Haarlem was paid to keep out dogs which had followed their masters to church. He also roused the sleepy during the long sermons. In the parish accounts, we find: 'To the Dogwhipper's sallery 1807, 10/-'.

On the pew ends we find curious representations of creatures such as a fierce looking goat tethered to a peg with a strong chain, and a dromedary with a Saracen [20] brandishing a scimitar on its back. The latter is particularly fanciful, although there is a mention in the early Churchwardens' accounts of a small sum being paid for seeing a dromedary which was passing through the township. Maybe the local craftsmen relied on memory, hearsay, or on the tales of returning travellers. Beyond the Dog-Whippers' Pew [21] is the Churchwardens' Pew which is beautifully crafted of old oak. Here you will find carvings of a unicorn, a monkey, and implements of the Passion.

3

THE MOCK CORPORATION PEW

The Mock Corporation of Sefton was of a purely social character, formed primarily for the purpose of social intercourse with one another on the Sabbath Day. It was established by Liverpool gentlemen and merchants although some of its earliest members appear to have been customs officers, who would be familiar with the shore around Seaforth and Bootle Bay. Apart from eating and drinking copiously, they talked politics, bet on favourite horses and sometimes were attended upon by a band of musicians.

The earliest date in connection with the origins of the Corporation is a meeting, probably at Sefton, on 15th October 1753, but Officers were already in place by that date. On 11th November 1753 there was a meeting 'held at Philip Syers alias Baxter Bor. in Order to fill up the vacant offices' and on 21st December 1753 there was 'A Council being held at Baxters Borough'. Baxters was a licensed premises on Great Crosby Marsh in Down Litherland (Seaforth), which is clearly marked on William Yates' and George Perry's map of 1768.

The centre of activities was the Church Inn [22] (situated at the western edge of the churchyard at that time) and the Punch Bowl and in the late afternoon, most members attended the evening service at Sefton Church, which they called 'The Cathedrall'. They possessed regalia [23], consisting of two large maces and two small ones, a sword, wands, cocked hats, and gowns, and a silver oar; the earliest mace bears the inscription, 'The gift of F. Cust, Esq., 1764'.

The main records begin in 1771 with meetings held exclusively at Sefton until 1772 when winter meetings were held at the Bootle Coffee House from 18th October until the middle of May. Mr Joseph Mayer, (1803–1886) the famous Liverpool antiquarian, named 'Bootle Mills' a favourite resort of artists from London spending their summers in the north, and Dr William Moss in his 'Liverpool Guide' of 1797 calls Bootle a place 'where genteel company resort for sea bathing and sea air in the summer season'. In a small book there are lists of members until 1829.

In 1881, two papers were read at the Historical Society of Lancashire and Cheshire by Englebert Horley, which stated that the whole of the regalia had been sold for £41 to the Bear's Paw Restaurant in Liverpool, except for the portrait of the Recorder [24] and a few pewter plates formerly used by the Corporation. These later became popular exhibits on display in the Liverpool Museum until they were sadly destroyed by enemy action during the night of 3rd–4th May 1941.

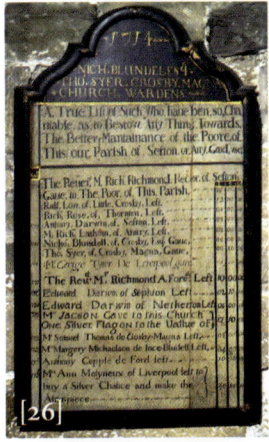

The Mock Corporation Pew (made by Robert Tyrer in 1772) is still extant with its three rows for the Burgesses and a separate square box [25] for the Mayor, and thanks to Caröe their principal records still exist.

The Rothwell Window

Behind the pews is the fine west window of the North Aisle, the masonry of which is late fifteenth century. It was dedicated to the Marquess De Rothwell (Richard R. Rothwell 1809–1890) in 1895.

[28]

North Aisle

On the north wall, above the pew, is the Benefactors' Board [26], placed here under the instruction of Nicholas Blundell, Church Warden 1714–15 and Squire of Little Crosby.

4

THE NORTH DOOR

Above the north door is a beautiful memorial group in marble [27] designed by a young John Gibson, and dedicated to Henry Blundell of Ince Hall. Before Gibson studied in Rome and became a Royal Academician, he was an apprentice in Liverpool to Messrs. Franceys. The white marble group represents the deceased relieving Genius and Poverty. Henry Blundell was the renowned antiquarian who assembled the fine collection of marble statues, now mainly residing in the Walker Art Gallery, Liverpool. It is said that the verse was composed by William Roscoe, MP for Liverpool and famous philanthropist and writer.

Memorial to Henry Blundell of Ince

To the MEMORY of

Henry Blundell Esq.,

of Ince Blundell in the County of LANCASTER;

Who died August 28th. 1810 aged 86.

MAY HE REST IN PEACE!

[29]

This is the door used for access to the north churchyard and it may have been used by members of the Mock Corporation to sneak into the service late from their repast at the Church Inn.

It appears to be the original fifteenth-century door, and on the outside there are the remains of what could be a Sanctuary Knocker [28]. Outlaws could claim asylum from the Church if they could reach such a knocker. Stratford upon Avon has a famous example.

To the right (east) of the north door is a fine stained glass window (detail of St Oswald) [29] commemorating two friends who died in World War II. John Paul Zacharias [30] and John H. Child Pearson [31].

The stonework of this mediaeval window (and the one to its right) has been recently restored.

[30]

Men of Sefton Cabinet

Here is a fine modern oak cabinet containing a book by Kay Slater describing the Men of Sefton who fought in the two world wars.

[31]

War Memorial

The War Memorial [32] (designed by Caröe) gives the dates 1914–1919. Even more unusually, it lists not only the men of Sefton Parish who died in the First World War, but also all who fought.

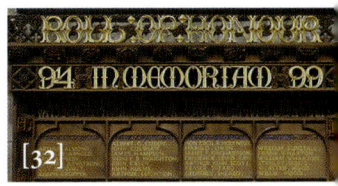

5

ROYAL COAT OF ARMS

On the wall above the War Memorial we have a painted board depicting a royal Coat of Arms. This denotes the fact that the monarch is the Supreme Governor of the Church of England. As monarchs change, so do coats of arms. This one appears to be the arms of William of Orange, but on his death in 1702, it seems to have been altered slightly to become the arms of Queen Anne. It was probably painted by a country artist and is in oil on rough boards. The lion [33] and the unicorn support the main shield which, according to the Rouge Dragon Pursuivant, is incorrect in one small detail. Anne chose the motto of Elizabeth I: *Semper Eadem* (Always the Same) which might have been painted over William's motto at the base.

The Audley Window: Te Deum

This window [34] was given by the children of William and Anne Audley in 1927. One of the children, George, was a great philanthropist and gave the two copies of old master paintings to the church.

Works of Mercy Window

The window which straddles both sides of the screen illustrates the Works of Mercy (in St Matthew's Gospel) and was the gift of Ellen Edwards in memory of her brother Thomas, of Abbey's Farm. He died on 14th January 1903.

6

HATCHMENTS AND MONUMENTS

Between the Audley Window and the Edwards Window there is a benefactors' board listing the legacies of Mrs Ann Molyneux, William Thompson Esq and Mr Robert Davenport. It commences with a huge legacy of £52 given by Mrs Ann Molyneux in 1728, the interest from which had to provide penny loaves to the poor of the townships of Sefton, Netherton and Lunt every Sunday.

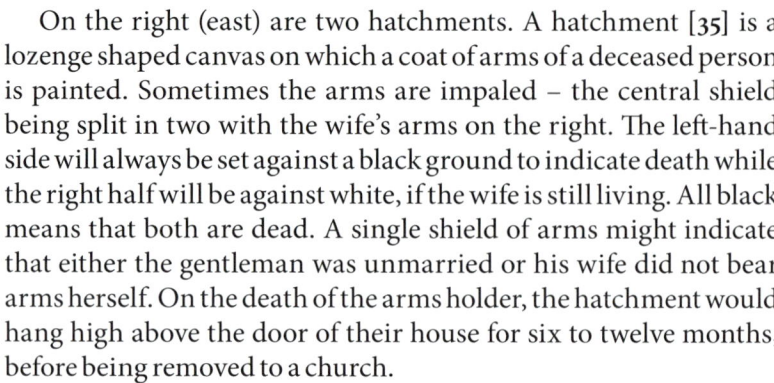

[35]

On the right (east) are two hatchments. A hatchment [35] is a lozenge shaped canvas on which a coat of arms of a deceased person is painted. Sometimes the arms are impaled – the central shield being split in two with the wife's arms on the right. The left-hand side will always be set against a black ground to indicate death while the right half will be against white, if the wife is still living. All black means that both are dead. A single shield of arms might indicate that either the gentleman was unmarried or his wife did not bear arms herself. On the death of the arms holder, the hatchment would hang high above the door of their house for six to twelve months, before being removed to a church.

The word is derived from the French achevèment and is similar in meaning to the English 'achievement' which is used in English heraldry.

The highest hatchment is that of Henry Blundell of Ince (1724–1810) the famous antiquarian whose monument by Gibson we have seen above the north door. He was married to Elizabeth, the daughter of Sir George Mostyn, fourth baronet of Talacre. As she died in 1767, the impaled arms are set against a black background. On the left are the arms of Blundell of Ince, with the ten billets with a Cornish chough or raven. The Mostyn arms are represented by ermine and ermines and a lion rampant. The Blundell motto has been replaced by a religious sentiment: SPES TUTISSIMA COELIS (*The safest hope is Heaven*). A skull at the base tells us that this is the end of a particular line – in this case the Blundells of Ince. Henry had become estranged from his son Charles Robert who had refused to marry and the latter bequeathed the manor of Ince to Thomas Weld, a distant relative.

The lower hatchment [36] is the earliest and most interesting in Sefton Church. It belongs to Nicholas Blundell the Diarist (died 1737). His shield of ten billets impale those of his surviving wife Frances, daughter of Lord Langdale (a chevron and three stars or estoiles). No motto is given but we might have expected to see: IN OMNIBUS REQUIEM QUAESIVI (*I sought peace in all things*), which Nicholas used frequently in his written work.

[36]

7

THE SCREENS AND CANOPIES

Some of the most impressive features of the church are its Tudor Screens and canopies – separating the nave from the Chancel and the side chapels. These were originally erected in the early sixteenth century. What we see today, however beautiful, is not what was originally created. Over the centuries, the screens have been moved, chopped up, allowed to fall apart, partly replaced and recreated. A great deal of detective work is required to understand how they have been transformed.

In the nineteenth century, there was a Royal Coat of Arms of Queen Victoria (1842) on top of the main screen, which no doubt replaced earlier royal arms. This screen was obviously constructed as a 'Rood Screen' – designed to support a crucifixion scene with Christ on the cross, flanked by Mary his mother and St John. We are not sure whether such a representation was ever placed here as the Reformation immediately followed the screen's construction. A closer examination of the carving on the screen will reveal many Renaissance ornaments such as 'putti' – showing that rural, remote Sefton was actually at the cutting edge of European design. This probably encouraged so-called 'restorers' between 1820–1843, who also lowered the screen, to replace the west-facing 'gothic' pointed arches with a renaissance-style rounded arcade, page 8, illustration [9]. Fortunately, Caröe in the early twentieth century was sensible and able enough to restore the screen to its original position and appearance which produces the pleasing effect originally intended.

[37]

The Shields

Looking up at the canopy, on the nave (west) side we can see an array of shields, [37 and 38] but only two – those with the 'Cross Moline' – are original. The others are of distinguished members of the Sefton family: Sir Richard of Navarett, Sir Robert of Bloreheath, and Sir William of Flodden with two of the standards he captured from the Scots. Some of the shields belong to allied families such as the Stanleys, Lathoms and Scarisbricks, and of Edward I and Eleanor of Castile. On the other side of the screen (east) are the shields of builders and rectors of the church and of Margaret Bulcley, and of the sitting and crouching hare – badges of the Molyneux family. The pendant angels on the west side are original, and bear the emblems of the Passion.

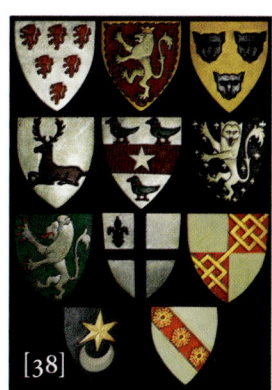

[38]

The Pulpit

Before the Reformation, the Altar was the focal point of a church building, but the reformers put the emphasis on the Word. The pulpit [39] (of 1635) became all-important and originally stood attached to the central pillar on the north side of the nave (note the fixing mark on the pillar). On the opposite pillar in the nave there are the remains of a fixing for a bracket whose purpose is unknown. In about 1820, (legal permission was granted in 1818), the pulpit was moved to a high position on the left of the door into the Chancel; subsequently it was reduced in height and moved further north to its present position. It is Jacobean, carved in florid renaissance style

[39]

[40]

and has two carved quotations from the Book of Proverbs. The Molyneux Pew had to be moved to the south aisle to accommodate the pulpit.

8

THE BLUNDELL CHAPEL

Going through the screen in the north aisle, we enter the Blundell Chapel, sometimes known as 'The Squire of Ince's Pew' [40]. The pew, which is enclosed by screens, was used by the early Blundells of Little Crosby,[4] and after the Reformation it was shared with the Blundells of Ince. Here the north wall dates partly from the fifteenth century and the join with later fifteenth-century work is clearly visible. The stalls on the north side have early Renaissance bench-ends, headed with the Tudor Rose instead of the usual poppy. The much later 'new' pews in the north and south aisles borrowed this design. Under the floor lie many Blundells, including William 'the Cavalier' (buried 1698) whose notes of his times form the basis of Rev T. E. Gibson's *A Cavalier's Note Book*. Nicholas Blundell [41], the Diarist (died 1737) is also buried here with his daughters Mary (1734) and Frances (1773), his grandsons William (died 1740), Christopher (died 1771 aged 35) and Nicholas (died 1795).

[41]

The white marble slab [42] was originally the top of an altar tomb in the same position but was reduced to floor level when the Blundell Pew was restored, the Chancel floor lowered and the south-east window restored by Capt Hon Richard Molyneux in 1919.

On the wall of the Blundell Chapel are monuments to the Blundell Family of Ince – Robert Blundell, C. R. Blundell, Elizabeth Blundell and Henry Blundell.

In the Blundell Chapel, there is a Memorial Book and oak case.

of M⁹ Mary Coppinger
ult 1734 aged 30 Years.
of Nicholas Blundell Esq
April 1736 aged 66 Years:
ly of William Blundell
740 aged 6 Months [42]

Teresa Booth

An interesting stone [43], which is partly found in the Blundell Chapel, gives us an insight into early surgical procedures:

> *Here lieth ye body of Mrs Teresa Booth who went to Wigan upon ye 28th of Octobr being St Simon and Judes day to have her breast cut for a cancer which was taken off ye 9th of Novbr and she died the 30th of Decbr 1717 in ye 42nd year of her age*
> *"Requiescat in Pace"*
> *She was housekeeper at Croxteth.*

Parish Chest

This fourteenth-century muniment chest [44] once held the parish records. It originally had three locks so that the Rector and the two

[43]

Churchwardens all had to be present with their keys in order to open it. This used to be sited in the Parvise Room (above the porch) which was called the Muniment Room.

Nicholas Blundell famously had it broken open:

> 21 April 1714 '… we caused a Chest over the Church Pourch to be brock open as had not ben open'd of very many years…'

[44]

9

THE LADY CHAPEL

Passing through the Blundell Chapel, we enter one of the oldest parts of the church which dates from the fourteenth century when the nave was much smaller and there was no south aisle. On the north wall, we are struck by many things, including the window, the painting, the hatchment and the effigies on the floor.

The Square-headed Window

The glass in this window was installed in 1901 in memory of Kathleen and Doreen, the infant daughters of John and Kathleen Gallaher. The original mediaeval glass was grisaille, with a border decorated with oak leaves, acorns and roses.

[45]

The Tuscan Madonna

This painting is a copy of the Madonna del Granduca, by Raphael. The original painting hangs in the Pitti Gallery (Pitti Palace) in Florence and is priceless and was probably painted in 1505, shortly after Raphael arrived in Florence. He was possibly influenced in his use of sfumato by seeing the great paintings of Leonardo Da Vinci there. Sfumato is the technique of toning down, or to evaporate like smoke. There are no harsh outlines, a famous example being Da Vinci's Mona Lisa. The original painting belonged to Ferdinand III Grand Duke of Tuscany, from whom it got its name.

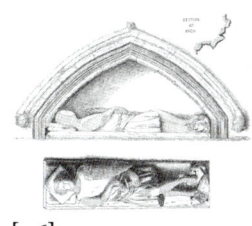

[46]

Hatchment

The large hatchment [45] displays the Molyneux coat of arms with the famous Cross Moline.

The Two Knight Effigies

One of the most interesting and intriguing aspects of the church is the pair of 'Crusader Knights' [46 and 47] now seen in the Lady Chapel. It is likely that they were originally painted (we know that they were later whitewashed), but apart from that we know little about them. These are not particularly rare – there are fine Stanley effigies in Ormskirk Church and a similar example depicts Sir Robert de Stiverton (1307) at Kildwick in Craven.

[47]

[48]

The figure in the canopied niche [46 and 48] holds a shield bearing the Cross Moline (the Molyneux cross) but wears no armour except genouillères, which would date it before the fourteenth century. It could possibly be Sir William Molyneux, who was made a knight banneret in Gascony in 1286 by the Earl of Lancaster. This effigy appears to be about 30–40 years older than its companion, i.e. about 1296–8. He was lying in this situation in 1822 as he was illustrated in Richard Bridgens' book that year.

The second effigy [47, 49 and 50] is less certain. There is no record and no Cross Moline nor sign of any kind whatsoever by which even his family can be identified. It is possible that the original paintwork included a Cross Moline which was accidentally removed with the whitewash. There is a clue in the *Illustrated Itinerary of Lancashire 1842* which states:

[49]

'By their armorial shields they are members of the same family.'

This would imply that the shield on the second effigy still bore traces of original paintwork in 1842.

Judging from his plate armour, we may safely assign his date to the early fourteenth century – 1325–40. The fact that this knight is bearded further confirms this date, as this was temporarily the fashion. Caröe asserts that the beard is the original one and was formerly covered by a false beard of cement.

[50]

 It is not improbable that the effigy is of the last Molyneux of Little Crosby, Sir John, by marriage with the daughter of whom (Agnes) the estate passed to David Blundell of Ainsdale. Notice the bent figure at the foot of the knight [49 and 50] – much worn now, but still retaining signs of having been originally a very fine piece of work.

Thomas Ashcroft, writing in 1819 says, 'Much of their beauty has been lost by that pernicious and simple custom of whitewashing'.[5]

10

MOLLINEX CHANTRY

[51]

When the church was rebuilt in the early sixteenth century, this earlier chapel was saved and its west wall opened out to create the North Aisle. Around the same time, it became the site of the Mollinex Chantry founded by Edward Molyneux in 1535 while the east end of the new south aisle had become the Chantry at the altar of Our Lady of Pity (founded by Margaret Bulcley about 1528).

In the walls of the Lady Chapel are the signs of a former pointed roof. The centrepiece of the Lady Chapel is the carved altarpiece [51], by Nathanial Hitch, given in 1918 by the Countess of Sefton as a memorial to her daughter. The ivory candlesticks were carved from the tusks of a rhinoceros – something anathema today.

Piscina

In the Lady Chapel, low on the east wall, there is a beautiful double piscina [52], which now has no drainage holes. It is obviously in its original position although the floor has been raised. As already noted, its tracery is of a similar design to the window in the tower. Above it, there used to be evidence of a shelf (for a statue?) and the faint memory of the remains of old plaster of a fresco with folds of a trailing robe visible in the nineteenth century. The Latin name *piscina* originally meant a fish pond.

[52]

Charles William 3rd Earl of Sefton

To the right of the altarpiece on the wall is a monument to Charles William 3rd Earl of Sefton [53] who died on 2nd August 1855 aged 59. For many years it was hidden behind the Lady Chapel altarpiece, and has recently been relocated further to the south. Charles William is buried in a vault under the Lady Chapel and his funeral was an event of monumental proportions as his body was brought from Croxteth Hall to Sefton Church.

[53]

Choir Vestry and Revestry

Beyond the canopied knight is a door cut through in 1915 to the 'new' Choir Vestry, which had a kitchen and WC added in the late twentieth century. Now indoors, the original sixteenth-century external buttress is visible. Beyond this Vestry is the Revestry – built in 1540 by Anthony Molyneux. Here its north door and south window have been swapped so that access is now internal. From the Revestry, there is a modern wooden staircase and door cut through the east wall of the Chancel to give direct access to the church. In earlier times the priest must have walked around the front of the church and entered through the porch – even in the rain and snow.

11

THE CHANCEL

This is one of the glories of the church and is part of the 'new' building by the Molyneux family in the early sixteenth century.

[54]

Aumbry

On the north wall we see the Aumbry [54 and 55] – with its beautifully carved ogee arch and later, plainer door. Its finial has been replaced at some stage. Some historians have suggested that this could be an Easter Sepulchre. The Parish Registers were kept here until they were deposited at the Lancashire Archives in Preston

[55]

[56]

where they are preserved in a strictly controlled environment. The Registers start relatively early (1597) as they were only ordered to be kept in 1541. It is possible that even earlier registers were destroyed during the Reformation.

Sedilia

On the south wall there is a fine set of Sedilia. These were seats for the priests, with the most easterly one reserved for the most important cleric present. These are now far too high to be used, but we know that the Chancel floor was lowered in 1919. In the east corner of the Sedilia is the Credence, where the sacred vessels and elements would rest. The stone [56] high on the west side is said to be where the priest sharpened the arrows brought to be blessed before battle, although this was possibly a reused stone from the exterior of the earlier building. Other internal stones have been found with definitive evidence of external use.

[57]

The Reredos (1732)

In the early eighteenth century, the church was 'modernised' and part of this scheme was a new classical reredos, which is simple yet dramatic. Set in the centre of dark wood panelling is a later gilded wooden sunburst, with the sacred Christogram IHS in the centre. The letters refer to Iesus Hominum Salvator, Jesus Saviour of mankind. Reverence for the holy name of Jesus goes back to the earliest days of Christianity, and after the Reformation both Luther and Calvin promoted such devotion. While the reredos was given by Mrs Ann Molyneux[6] of Liverpool in 1732 (see Benefactors' Board), the gilded host with its dramatic sunburst rays [57] was added in 1820.

On the right hand side of the reredos is the modern door to the Revestry, which is disguised in the panelling.

[58]

High Altar

The free-standing altar is early twentieth century (designed by Caröe), and made of wood. An earlier altar was given to a daughter church, and the mediaeval altar would have stood against the east wall below the great window. On the front (west) face of the altar is a seventeenth-century wooden shield of the Passion [58], which originated in Rouen. Belonging to Dr Longford, the Rector, it was fixed on the altar frontal during the restoration of 1935–37.

12

THE EAST WINDOW

The East Window [59]

This was given in 1870 in memory of Rev R. R. Rothwell, Rector. The remains of the previous window are in the Molyneux (south) Chapel and in the south aisle windows. There are two rows of main lights which mix Old and New Testament stories, with Christ as the centrepiece of the top row. There are also stags' heads and arms (of Rothwell), and scenes relating to St Helen and her son Constantine.

Sentence Boards

The East Window is now flanked on either side by two huge painted boards which for many years were displayed in the base of the tower. They have recently been returned to their original position. In 1603, the Creed and the Ten Commandments were ordered to be displayed on the east wall of all churches. These 'Sentences' date from 1707, and their paintwork has been restored.

Memorials

There are various interesting memorials on the walls of the Sanctuary and Chancel.

Rev Edward Morton

Rev Edward Morton has a beautiful monument [60] with a Latin inscription on the north wall of the Sanctuary. It tells how he was ejected from his Living during the Commonwealth period, then restored.

> *Here lyeth ye body of ye Reverend Edward Morton Dr in Divinity*
> *& late Rector of Sephton who departed this life Feb ye 28 1674*
> *Margaret Moreton Relict of Edward Moreton D.D June 30 Anno*
> *Dom 1694.*

Rothwell Monument and Hatchments

An impressive marble memorial [61] may be seen on the north wall of the Chancel erected by Rector Richard Rothwell [62] and dedicated in 1844 to fourteen members of his family. Many of them, including the Rector himself, are buried beneath the monument.

Two impressive hatchments belonging to the Rothwells can be seen high up on either side of the Chancel.

[63]

Rev Richard Rainshaw Rothwell, Rector of Sefton:

Sacred to the memory of the Hon. Richard Rainshaw Rothwell MA for 50 years Rector of this parish born January 27th 1771, died April 25th 1863.
Richard Rainshaw Rothwell, Marquis De Rothwell and Martha Lydiard, Marchioness de Rothwell
Sacred to the memory of Martha Lydiard, Marchioness de Rothwell Born 5th January 1821 fell asleep 28th June 1885
"Blessed are the dead which die in the Lord" Rev. XIV 13
And of Richard Rainshaw Rothwell Marquis de Rothwell who died March 11th 1890 aged 81 years.

Rev Anthony Halsall

Here lyeth the body of the Reverend Anthony Halsall late master of ye Free School of Great Crosby A native of ye Isle of Man and dedicated there to ye ministry of Christ [63]

[64]

He came early to England on ye express errand of supporting the rights of his church and country together with his truly Christian Diocesan D Thomas Wilson by whom he was singularly beloved at which time his personal merit unexpectedly recommended him to ye office which he filled at Crosby 25 years with integrity general esteem and success fitted for his important task by an uncommon strength and firmness of mind and an unwearied zeal to advance ye interests of religion by gentleness by reproof by instruction but above all by example.

The Choir

In the lower area of the Chancel is the Choir [64]. There are sixteen stalls raised on stone pierced with quatrefoils. They belong to the same period as the side screens which were originally canopied – 1500. The Rector's Stall and that opposite have chords and tassels carved on the desk ends and bear the inscription: 'I.M.' [65]. This, no doubt, refers to James Molyneux, Rector 1489–1509. This is a delightful area where one can find rabbits, hares [66] and a mobbed owl [67]. There is also a carved eagle which may refer to the arms of the Cotton family to whom Anthony Molyneux's mother belonged.

[65]

In the Choir Stalls at the north-east end is a 'Treacle Bible' (1596) sitting in a suitable oak and glass case. In 1541 by order of Henry VIII, an English Bible had to be 'set and fixed' in every church (which probably meant a chained bible). Unfortunately, in 1802 when funds were low, the Churchwardens sold off the old bible for £2 7s. An Old Folio New Testament Commentary later took its place until 1932 when Mr Raymond Richards gave the current bible which got its name from the infamous line in Jeremiah 8:22 which

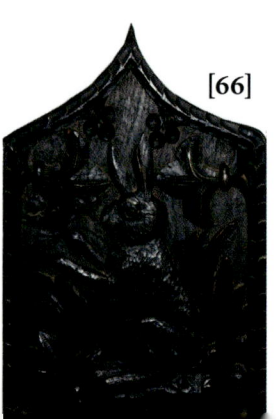
[66]

reads 'Is there not tryacle [treacle] at Gilead?' Modern translations use the word 'balm'. Other curious renderings occur at Psalm 91.5: 'Thou shalt not be afraid of eny bugges by night', and Isaiah 24.9: 'the beer shal be byter to them that drink it'.

In the eighteenth century through to the early nineteenth century, there are frequent references in the Churchwardens' Accounts to music which indicated the existence of a mixed choir and a rustic band. In 1763 there was a payment to 'the male singers', a bassoon was purchased in 1768 at a cost of £5 12s, and a hautboy, a base viol and a 'Clarenett' are mentioned. Sometimes singers from Douglas (Parbold), Kirkby, Aughton and Altcar visited, as well as instrumentalists – and none went home empty handed. The rustic band would have played in the west gallery.

[67]

The Church now has a robed mixed Choir which sings in the Chancel. It is affiliated to the Royal School of Church Music.

The Organ

The original Organ was built by the Liverpool firm Bewsher and Fleetwood in 1829 and was on a gallery at the west end of the Church. The organ in the Chancel was a rebuilding and enlarging of the 1828 instrument by William Hill of London in 1893. Its case is a beautiful example of 'modern' carving though in keeping with the older work. The case (1918), together with the cost of rebuilding and enlarging the organ, was the gift of Sir Robert Connell in memory of his son who died while still at Harrow. It was enlarged by Harrison and Harrison in 1922 and it was completely overhauled by Willis in 2007 with electro pneumatic action and computerisation and is a high quality instrument [68].

[68]

The Lectern

This modern piece of work in oak in medieval pattern was designed by Mr H. Rowse, FRIBA, and the gift of Mr and Mrs Herbert Jackson, 1937. Standing next to it is a fine oak book display case to complement the lectern. This was commissioned by the Friends of Sefton and presented in 2014. It displays a copy of Richard Bridgens' rare folio book, 'Sefton Church' (1822–1835) kindly donated by Mr Peter Mountfield.

The oak Litany Desk, in the centre of the Church commemorates the Coronation of Queen Elizabeth II in 1953. The church commissioned its companion desk in 2013 to mark her Golden Jubilee.

13

PAIR OF ALTAR TOMBS

Johanna Molyneux

[69]

[70]

On either side of the Chancel, we find an altar tomb separating it from the Lady Chapel and the Molyneux Chapel.

On the Lady Chapel side (north) the tomb is capped by an alabaster slab inscribed with the name of Johanna [69, 70, 71 and 72], wife of Sir Richard Molyneux, who distinguished himself at Agincourt and was knighted by Henry V in 1415. Sir Richard was further rewarded by Henry VI in 1446 by being granted the Chief Forestership of the royal forests in the Wapentake of West Derbyshire, the stewardship of West Derbyshire and also Salford. He and his heirs were also invested as Constables of Liverpool and Croxteth Park.

The monument to Johanna is much defaced, probably by school boys as this part of the church was once used as a schoolroom. Strangely, she lies alone.

The Latin inscription, partly illegible, is translated as:

> *Here lies Lady Johanna, formerly wife of Peter Legh, knight, and afterwards wife of Molyneux, knight, who was lady of Bradley Haydock, freeholder of part of the villages of Warrington, Great Sankey, and Burtonwood, lady of diverse portions of lands and holding between the towns of Newton, Goldborne, Lowton, Bolde, and Walton in the Dale, who died during the Feast of St Sulpice bishop, in the year of our Lord 1439, whose soul God pardon. Amen.*

[71]

One of their sons, Sir Richard, married Elizabeth, daughter of Thomas, Lord Stanley of Lathom, Lord Lieutenant of Ireland, and sister of Thomas, 1st Earl of Derby. Richard junior was held in such high esteem at Court that he received a special mention in the Act of Resumption (36 Hen VI) which states, 'Provided always that this Act extend not nor in any way be prejudicial unto Richard Molyneux Esq. of Sefton ...'. He sadly fell fighting under the Lancastrian banner at the bloody battle of Bloreheath, Staffordshire in 1459.

[72]

A notable brother of Richard, of Agincourt fame, appears in a different theatre of war – this time fighting the Saracens and Turks for the Cross. We have a record from 4th August 1448 which states that Sir Robert Molyneux (of Altcar) had been captured and forced to serve cruel men and confined in a castle called Topham, in bondage of the Great Marrot, 'who calls himself the Lord of all Turkey'. He was tortured in every way possible in the hope that he would renounce his Christian faith, but to no avail. He was then freed, but his two brothers retained as hostages, while he was given one hundred days to raise 1008 ducats. For every day late, his captives promised to cut off a limb of one of his brothers.

Yet another distinguished brother was Adam, Bishop of Chichester (1445) who also held the offices of Keeper of the Privy Seal to Henry VI and Clerk to the Privy Council. He was murdered at Portsmouth on 9th January 1450 while preparing to sail to France. It is said that a party of sailors executed him at the instigation of Richard Duke of York, but this might be a Tudor myth.

Sir Richard Molyneux and his Family, 1558

Across the Chancel on the south side, formerly the Bulcley Chantry, dissolved in 1546/8, we find an altar tomb [73] under the screen separating the Chapel from the Chancel; the Brasses represent Sir Richard Molyneux and his family, 1558 [74]. The quaint inscription at the foot of the knight, which sadly is not unique, reads:

> *Dame Worshoppe was my guide in lyfe*
> *and did my doings guyde*
> *Dame Wertue left me not alone*
> *when soule from bodye hyed*
> *And thoughe that deathe with dinte of darte*
> *hath brought my corps on sleape*
> *The eternall God my eternalle soule*
> *eternally doethe kepe*

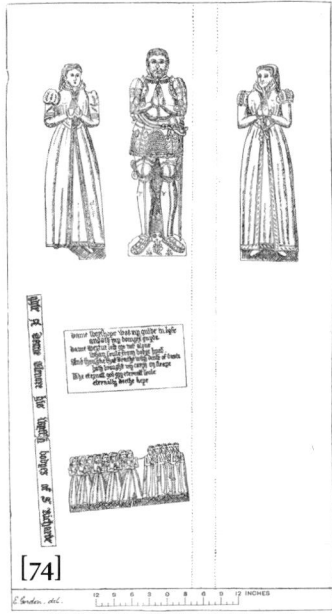

BRASS OF SIR RICHARD MOLYNEUX, 1558

The brass, which is set into the top of a quatrefoiled pedestal and is missing part of the inscription, reads, *Ye bodies of Sir Richard Molyneux knighte and Dame Elenore his wyffe.*

In fact, Sir Richard has two wives with him and their effigies are shown on the brass: Eleanor Radcliffe, daughter of Sir Alexander Radcliffe of Ordsall, and Eleanor Maghull, daughter of Robert Maghull of Maghull. Sir Richard, who built the great Tithebarn in Liverpool in a street still retaining that name, was knighted at the coronation of Queen Mary, and was made Sheriff of Lancashire in 1556 and died in 1558.

The thirteen children of the first marriage are shown on their mother's side – eight girls and five boys. Sadly, his six children with his second wife (five boys and one girl) are missing from the brass. He was an executor of Anthony Molyneux's Will (dated 13th October 1553) and alarmingly given: '. . . fulle auctoryte and power w'out scrouple of conscyence to adde to mynnyshe and chaunge any pt of this my wyll at there pleasure as they shall thinke most mette and convenyent'.

14

THE MOLYNEUX CHAPEL

[75]

In earlier guide books, this chapel was incorrectly identified as the site of the Molyneux (or Mollinex) Chantry, which we now know was situated in the Lady Chapel. Today, this chapel contains many memorials to the Molyneux family.

The South East Window

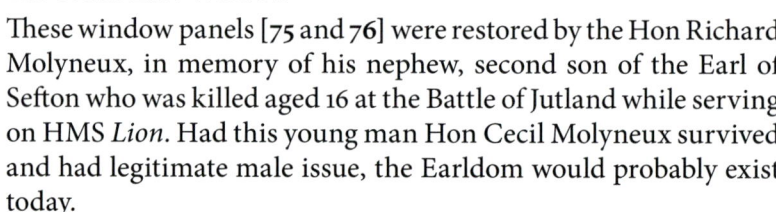

[76]

These window panels [75 and 76] were restored by the Hon Richard Molyneux, in memory of his nephew, second son of the Earl of Sefton who was killed aged 16 at the Battle of Jutland while serving on HMS *Lion*. Had this young man Hon Cecil Molyneux survived and had legitimate male issue, the Earldom would probably exist today.

Caryll Viscount Molyneux (white marble table tomb)

[77]

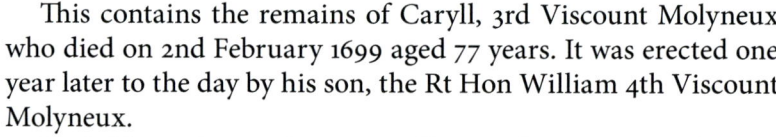

In this area of the church there are some interesting Molyneux monuments [80 and 81]. The white marble altar tomb [78] is the most dramatic as it displays a bas-relief carving of the Molyneux shield: the Sefton Cross Moline, supported by two lions and surmounted by a viscount's coronet. Below is the motto: VIVERE SAT VINCERE, translated as either *To conquer is to live enough* or *To live is conquering enough*. Below is an hourglass, a femur bone and a skull.

This contains the remains of Caryll, 3rd Viscount Molyneux who died on 2nd February 1699 aged 77 years. It was erected one year later to the day by his son, the Rt Hon William 4th Viscount Molyneux.

[78]

Buried here also are his son, William, 4th Viscount Molyneux who died on 8th of March, 1717, in the 62nd year of his age, Richard, 6th Viscount Molyneux who died on 12th December 1738, in his 60th year and Richard's wife Mary who died on 19th March 1766 aged eighty-six. Caryll became the third Viscount, but despite service to the Crown as Lord Lieutenant of Lancashire under King James II, he was later outlawed by parliament on account of his Faith. At length, by paying a massive fine, he regained possession, and lived to a great age. James II had constituted him Lord-Lieutenant and *custos rotulorum* (keeper of the rolls) of the County of Lancaster, and Admiral of the Narrow Seas. He died at Croxteth, 2nd February 1698/9, aged seventy-seven and was buried at Sefton, leaving three sons and five daughters, by Mary, daughter of Alexander Barlow of Barlow Esq.

[79]

The name Caryll (Carolus is Latin for Charles) is worthy of note as it derives from the surname of several of his maternal ancestors. Caryll's mother was Mary Caryll of Bentone and an earlier ancestor was Bridgett Carrell of Warnham, Sussex (sixteenth century). Caryll's older brother Sir Richard married Frances Seymour Caryll, daughter of the Duke of Somerset, but died without issue.

Briget Molyneux (*Black Table Tomb*)

Next to this tomb is a handsome black marble tomb [80]. In the centre panel is a coat of arms with three Luces (pikes), surrounded by scroll and leaves and surmounted by a coronet. It is the tomb of Briget Lucy of Charlecote in Warwickshire, who was the wife of William, the 4th Viscount (died 1717).

Nicholas Blundell of Crosby records the funeral in his Diary:

1713 May 5th. I met ye Corps of my Lady Molin: at Ormsk: and attended it to ye Funerall at Sefton, there was Sr Wm Gerard, Mr. Standish, Mr. Roger Diconson etc.

The inscription reads:

Here lyes interr'd ye Body of the Right Honourable BRIGET LADY Viscountes MOLYNEUX Daughter and heires of ROBERT LUCY Esq of Charlcote in the Country of Warwick and late wife of the Right Honourable WILLIAM LORD Viscount MOLYNEUX, who departed this life in ye 58th year of her age on ye 23rd day of April Anno Domini 1713.
Requiescat in pace.

Here lieth the Body of the Right Honourable Caryl Lord Viscount Molyneux who departed this life the 11th of November 1745 in the 62 year of his Age ✠ may his Soule rest in Peace.

The arms of the Lucy family are featured here – with the three pikes (or luces) haurient [82] – that is with their heads out of the water. Arms were originally used on the field of battle so the design would often be a pun on the name – as an aid to memory. It is thought that the Lucys originated in the village of Lucé in Normandy.

There is a local legend that the young William Shakespeare was once caught poaching deer on the Charlecote estate and brought before Sir Thomas Lucy in the Great Hall. It is said that he later took revenge by modelling the fussy Justice Shallow in *Henry IV pt 2* and *The Merry Wives of Windsor* on Sir Thomas. Thomas, as an ardent supporter of the new religion, had also been a great persecutor of Shakespeare's Catholic relatives, so possibly the story of antagonism contains some truth. The Lucy family became extinct in the male line and the Estate is now owned by the National Trust.

Elizabeth Sherburne (brass on floor)

This brass tells a sad tale.

> *Here lyeth Elizabeth the fifth daughter of Sr Ric Mollinex Knight and Barronett who married Richard Sherburne son and Heyre apparent of Richard Sherburne of Stonihurst in the Countie of Lancaster Esqr the 19th October 1613 and was delivered of a daughter 30th of June 1615 and died in childbed the 3 of July next ensuing which daughter was named Elizabeth who died on Christmas days in the same year 1615.*

15

SIR WILLIAM MOLYNEUX

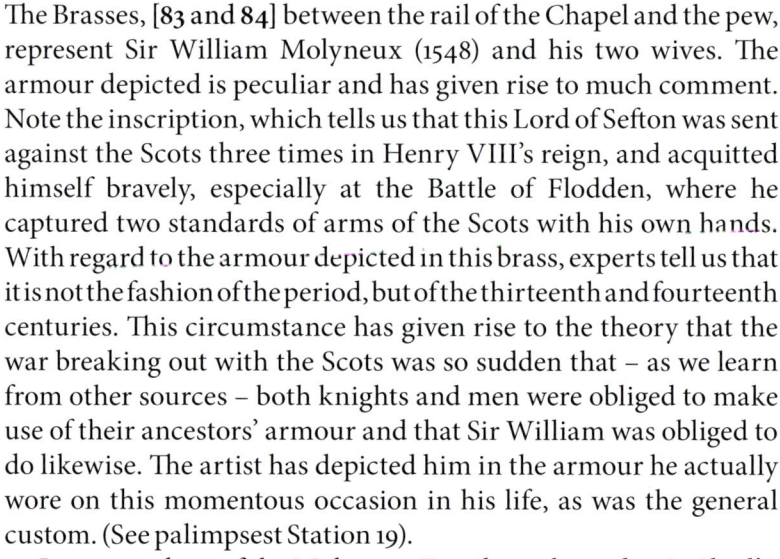

[83]

The Brasses, [83 and 84] between the rail of the Chapel and the pew, represent Sir William Molyneux (1548) and his two wives. The armour depicted is peculiar and has given rise to much comment. Note the inscription, which tells us that this Lord of Sefton was sent against the Scots three times in Henry VIII's reign, and acquitted himself bravely, especially at the Battle of Flodden, where he captured two standards of arms of the Scots with his own hands. With regard to the armour depicted in this brass, experts tell us that it is not the fashion of the period, but of the thirteenth and fourteenth centuries. This circumstance has given rise to the theory that the war breaking out with the Scots was so sudden that – as we learn from other sources – both knights and men were obliged to make use of their ancestors' armour and that Sir William was obliged to do likewise. The artist has depicted him in the armour he actually wore on this momentous occasion in his life, as was the general custom. (See palimpsest Station 19).

Later members of the Molyneux Family are buried at St Chad's, Kirkby:

Mary Augusta (1818–1906) widow of 3rd Earl
William Philip (1835–1897) (4th Earl)
Charles William Hylton (1867–1901) (5th Earl)
Osbert Cecil (1871–1930) (6th Earl)
Hugh William Osbert (1898–1972) (7th and last Earl) [85]

Monument at Kirkby to Cecil Richard Molyneux (1899–1916)

> *In Memory of Midshipman the Honble Cecil Richard Molyneux RN second son of Osbert 6th Earl of Sefton and of Helena his wife born December 2 1899 fell in action May 31 1916 in the battle of Jutland buried at sea*
> *As gold in the furnace hath he tried them.*

[84]

[85]

On the wall there is a modern memorial [86] (with the Cross Moline) placed in 1980 on the death of the last Countess, commemorating the Molyneux family's long association with this church.

Below it is a large stone found in the rectory garden with the Molyneux coat of arms. It may have originally come from Sefton Hall.

[86]

Fragments of Masonry

On the floor are pieces of masonry and tiles [87] recovered during various nineteenth-century restorations of the church. It was from these fragments of the original building that the date AD 1170 was settled upon. Note the fragment of a thirteenth-century priest's tombstone, the two lines being the stem of a cross, at the side of which is carved a chalice.

16

MARGARET BULCLEY

[87]

The Sefton Corporation Pew

The village of Sefton has given its name to the large Metropolitan Borough which stretches from Bootle in the south to Southport in the north. This beautifully carved enclosed pew contains the fine brass of Margaret Bulcley, 1528; both have been removed from the west side of the screen to their present position and there is evidence that the pew screen was originally sited on the west side of the Blundell Pew until 1818.

Margaret Bulcley 1528 (brass on floor)

This is now usually protected by a covering and can be found immediately inside the pew. Margaret faces us wearing a long plain dress with a small collar and wide-cuffed sleeves. She wears a pedimented headdress, and a girdle around her waist. Around her neck hangs a small chain bearing the T-shaped cross of St Anthony and her hands are joined in prayer. The whole figure is set within a double canopy with pillars at the sides. There are Tudor or Lancaster roses and arms on the shields of Molyneux and Bulcley (right) and Dutton and Molyneux (left [88]). Unfortunately the original coloured enamel has perished. A brass at Childwall Church of Henry Norris (died 1524) shows his wife Clemence wearing an identical girdle, although she wears an outer cloak [89] (seen on right of illustration).

[88]

[89]

South East Window

This is a delightful window which contains collected fragments from the old East Window [77 and 79] with figures telling the story of the Salutation (Mary's Visitation to her cousin Elizabeth, the mother of John the Baptist [90]). Luckily these shards have been carefully gathered and reused. It is a riot of mediaeval figures and colour, with a dismembered hand floating above. The Latin inscription of the original east window is reproduced as:

> *Pray for the good estate of Richard Molyneux, Knight, who had this window made in the year of Our Lord 1551.*

[90]

Worthies' Window

The Window behind the Pew, designed by the former Rector, Dr W. W. Longford, commemorates Dr Anthony Molyneux (Rector 1535–57), and depicts figures of famous Oxford churchmen of the early sixteenth century. It was obviously conceived to celebrate the 400th anniversary of Anthony Molyneux's rectorship at Sefton, with a touch of vanity with the reference to Magdalen College, Oxford which Rector Longford attended. The inscription reads:

> *To commemorate A. Molineux rector of this church; Fellow of the contemporary Oxford Churchmen.*

This window, a pet project of Dr Longford in 1936, was no doubt controversial when it was installed, especially as Thomas More was canonised a Saint of the Roman Church in 1935 and Cardinal Wolsey [91] stands in his scarlet robes as a Prince of the Church (he was Papal Legate from 1518 to his death). Dr Longford felt the need to write an explanation of the window, 'for the benefit of those who did not hear the Rector's account from the pulpit of the historical significance of the churchmen commemorated in the new window' (1936).[7] The Rector explains at length that, 'all were members of the Church of England. They were not Roman Catholics'. He continues by describing the characters in the window as, 'leaders in what is known as the New Learning'.

In our more enlightened times, we can appreciate this window for what it is, and not worry whether English Churchmen were Catholics or Anglicans. Incidentally, Thomas More appears in another unexpected place – on a monument to the Russian Revolution in the grounds of the Kremlin in Moscow. Dr Longford notes that the Sefton window was given by an 'anonymous' donor, which was later revealed to be Sir Benjamin Johnson (died 25th December 1937) of Messrs Johnson Brothers, the dyeing firm.

[91]

The window depicts the following people:

Top row (from left to right)
Anthony Molineux T. D., William Wareham, Thomas Wolsey, Thomas More.
Second Row (from left to right)
John Colet [92], Richard Fox, Thomas Linacre, William Grocyn.

17

SOUTH AISLE WINDOWS

There are three windows in the South Aisle. These were re-illuminated in 1937 with figurative representations of William and Margaret Bulcley, Laurence and Helen Ireland, and of Sir Alexander and Agnes Osbaldeston of the Edge, Sefton. All three, like the one behind the Molyneux Pew, were constructed by Mr H. G. Hiller to the design of Dr Longford.

William and Margaret Bulcley 1543 (east, but the original lights were in the centre) [93].

Laurence and Helen Ireland 1540 (centre).

Sir Alexander and Agnes Osbaldeston of the Edge, Sefton (west). The original inscriptions are to be found at the base of the windows. In the lower lights there are square fragments of old windows. Beneath Margaret Bulcley is the symbol of St Mark. Beneath the Ireland window are an 'M' for Molyneux and a Cross Moline, and under the Osbaldestons are the symbols of SS Luke and John [94]. Sadly St Matthew is missing.

It is interesting in that we can date the original windows, and therefore an approximate date of the rebuilding of the nave. The original Ireland window was made in 1540 and the Bulcley window in 1543.

[94]

Fixed on a seat below the Bulcley window there used to be a brass plate with a Latin inscription which read:

Pray for the soul of Margaret, daughter of Sir Richard Molyneux, wife 1st, of John Dutton, Esq., and 2dly, of William Buckley, Esq., who having founded here a perpetual chantry, and endowed it with rents and lands for one chaplain for ever, to celebrate divine service for the souls of Margaret, her relations and benefactors; died 21st February, 1528.

(quoted in Baines' *History of Lancashire*).

Rectors' List: Mortuary Slab

The List of Rectors of Sefton, to be seen on a slate slab [95] below the first of these windows, was inscribed by Mr Eric H. Banner, Church-warden. This slab has its own interesting, if gruesome, history. Originally it was used in the mortuary which was situated at the edge of the west churchyard to lay out bodies recovered from nearby beaches and the River Alt.

The Pews, running up to the south wall, are twentieth-century and correspond to those on the north side.

Skaters in Sefton Meadows

This delightful oil painting [96 and **cover**] depicts a winter scene to the north east of the church. Every winter, the meadows flooded and, in extreme cold temperatures, froze. This provided free entertainment for people, who flocked from the whole district to enjoy skating. In the twentieth century, the river was diverted into a new course, with flood controls.

A pen and ink drawing of an earlier date has recently come to light in Winchester and has been kindly lent by Dilly Hayman for this publication (page 39).

Robert Thompson Table

The huge oak table in this area is used for signing the marriage register and other events. It has the characteristic carved mouse which is waiting for you to find. Robert Thompson (1876–1955) lived in Kilburn, North Yorkshire, where the Parish Church is furnished with mice and one of the largest ongoing commissions is at Ampleforth Abbey and College.

18

PEW ENDS

One of the most characteristic features of this church is its wood-carving, particularly its pew ends. These are contemporary with the rebuilding of the nave (early sixteenth-century) and include a variety of symbols as well as a curiously designed alphabet (omitting W, X and Z). It is worth just wandering around the pews and examining one or two at leisure. On the north side of the main aisle we can find a mitre and chalice [97]; a curious carved head of a man; a colt; a displayed eagle; a pomegranate; a cross and nails; a cross and crown of thorns; a cross with spear and reed; a cross with hammer and pincers; a cock on a pedestal; a cross with scourges. These last six represent the instruments of the Passion and have

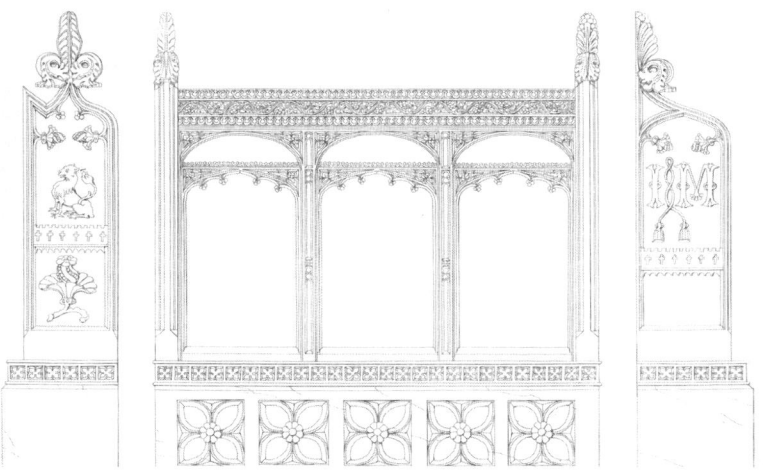

South side of the Choir.

[99]

been used in churches since the Middle Ages. There are also versions of the Cross Moline (Molyneux Cross), roses, vines, fruit, flowers and other foliage. Caröe suggests that the workmen were thoroughly enjoying themselves, and Ashcroft noted, 'I have oftentimes seen, on visiting antient religious edifices, strangely carved fancies of the over-witty workmen, that excite our risible faculties'.

The letters of the alphabet [98] ornament the pew ends in the nave. These are of an ingenious design which could resemble plaited corn. The missing letters remain a mystery – maybe some pew ends have been lost.

A puzzling pew end features the mitre and chalice or covered cup but this might be explained by the fact that a James Molyneux (Rector James Molyneux was also Archdeacon of Richmond) witnessed a deed in 1501 for the Mascy family which used a chalice/cup as an armorial device. John de Mascy was Rector of Sefton commencing in 1339.

The most strange carving of all in the church is the mysterious male head [99 and 100] which appears near the Blundell Chapel. This is the head and shoulders of a bearded man, looking straight ahead. He wears a tunic and a strange hat complete with feather. Below him are two sheaves of corn. It has been suggested that this is Christ, and the corn represents the Bread of Life. Caröe thought that it was clumsy and displeasing but this probably reflected his Victorian taste.

[100]

35

BOTTICELLI MADONNA

[101]

The painting in the huge handsome square frame at the west end of this wall is a print of the Botticelli Madonna [101] enclosed in a magnificent frame, presented (1927) – with the Raphael painting in the Lady Chapel – by Mr George Audley. The frame alone cost £200 at the time. The 'original' copy was destroyed by water damage.

Palimpsest – Thomas Hay of London

[102]

On the east side of the inner porch is a copy of the palimpsest [102] found on the reverse of the brass of Sir William Molyneux [84]. In October 1989, Sir William's brass was lifted for repair and restoration and another figure was revealed on the reverse. The brass containing the text was also found to have been reused. These are called palimpsests. It was not an uncommon practice for brass to be reused in this manner; after all, graves were reused after a suitable interval. Fortunately very little of our unknown man had to be cut away to provide the outline for Sir William. Our mystery man stands facing us in civilian dress of a fur-trimmed gown and a purse at his waist. He is clean shaven, has shoulder length hair and has long thin hands touching in prayer. It is thought to date from about 1500.

Fortunately, the palimpsest on the inscription plate clearly identifies a gentleman called Thomas Hay, a goldsmith who died in 1405. From his Will, which survives in the Guildhall, we know that he requested his burial in St Peter's Westcheap in London (now destroyed). We do know that the Molyneux brasses were made in London, probably from the London G series, but we do not know why used brasses were employed. Maybe the originals were rejected on artistic grounds, so simply remade on the reverse. Whatever the story, it is amazing that a London gentlemen should have resided unknown in Sefton Church, and for such a long period.

[103]

Now we are coming to the end of our tour, it is time to stand back and admire the church as a whole once more. Look up and see the fine bleached oak roofs [103] of the Chancel and nave which were completed in August 1909. The cross and monogram of St Helen, the Cross Moline, the Sacred Monogram (IHS) and the date were carved on the bosses. A fourteenth-century tie beam found in the old roof was retained by Caröe.

20

THE CHANDELIERS

We are fortunate to possess three large brass twelve-branch chandeliers [104] dating from 1773. Little is known of their fabrication but they were given by Richard de Rothwell, Rector and Patron. We do know that the church accounts show a payment of 2/- in 1820 for 'Carting Chandeliers from Canal' and in 1826, 21/- was paid for 'Gilding Doves on Chandeliers'.

The doves themselves are interesting. Made of wood and gilded, they show the birds in flight. The dove symbolised the Holy Spirit appearing over Christ's head at his baptism by John the Baptist, as told by Matthew 3:16. In a smoky, dusty environment the brass probably needed a clean every fifty years or so and would be shipped into Liverpool down the canal. Now they are lacquered and in pristine condition and probably look exactly like they did in 1773.

[104]

Fortunately, as electricity only came to Sefton Church in the early 1970s, the chandeliers were never converted, but always used for their original purpose – to shed light from real candles. Now we have the luxury of lighting them for special events such as Christmas services and Candlemas when they lend a mellow glow in an age of fluorescent tubing. Let them remind us that Jesus is the Light of the World.

Jacobean Texts

Notice the remains of texts [105] high up in the spandrels of the arches which were taken from Timothy, Corinthians, Matthew, Proverbs and the Lord's Prayer. These were uncovered when the whitewash was scrubbed off in 1891. These black-letter texts probably date from James I when an Order in Council demanded: *(that) all Popish ordinances and ornaments should be removed from the walls of churches, and suitable texts of Holy Scripture painted on the walls in place thereof.*

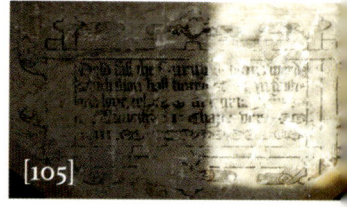

[105]

Some of the texts have been identified as follows:
North side:

Hold fast the form of sound words, which thou hast heard of me, in faith and love which is in Christ Jesus. 2 Timothy, chap I verse 13
This is a faithful saying, and worthy of all acceptation, that Christ Jesus came into the world to save sinners; of whom I am chief. 1 Timothy: chap 1 : verse 15
Now then we are ambassadors for Christ, as though God did beseech you by us; we pray you in Christ's stead, be ye reconciled to God. 2 Corinthians, chap 5, verse 20

South side:

> *Except your righteousness shall exceed the righteousness of the scribes and Pharisees, ye shall in no case enter into the kingdom of heaven. Matthew, chap 5, verse 20*

Robert Thompson Cupboard

The Church Shop by the door is lucky to store its stock in a classic Robert Thompson wardrobe, complete with mouse.

Bolshaw Window

Behind the shop table is the south west window which on a summer's evening is ablaze with colour. You will notice that the upper four lights seem of a different style and quality from the bottom row. The window is in memory of Elizabeth Bolshaw who died 8th April 1871. Work must have stopped when the bottom lights [106] were completed, for the window was finished off at a later date by Elizabeth Woodcock, her cousin. The bottom lights appear more formal, with the four Evangelists sitting writing their gospels, while the top scenes are clearly influenced by the Art Nouveau Movement. It is possible that two different firms were involved.

OUTSIDE THE CHURCH

After noting the stately spire with its peculiar 'beehive' turrets and the graceful proportions of the whole building from a distance, there are a number of objects of interest to be viewed:

The old Sundial

This early eighteenth-century sundial can be found in the south churchyard. There is also the base of the old village cross, near which the Rev G. W. Wall had his grave placed.

The old Buttress

This is one of the original fourteenth-century buttresses of the old church and can be found on the north side of the church at the east corner, adjoining the Vestry.

Churchyard Wall

It will be of interest to many to inspect the old churchyard wall facing the meadows: this was pierced with embrasures during the early part of the First World War, when the Mill Dam Bridge was guarded by sentries and heavily sandbagged and barbed-wired.

Early nineteenth-century pen and ink drawing
of Sefton Meadows in winter.

Courtesy of Dilly Hayman

The Sadler Memorial

An extract from the Rev G. W. Wall's paper before the Historical Society of Lancashire and Cheshire, 7th March, 1895, reads:

> In or about the year 1756 the art of printing on pottery from engraved copper plates was discovered by John Sadler of Liverpool, whose father, Adam Sadler, said to have served under Marlborough, established the Print House in Liverpool. Members of the family are commemorated by inscriptions on two grave-stones lying in the angle between the chancel and the south aisle on the exterior of the church.

Because of water damage, the original stones are becoming illegible and a new upright stone [107] has been placed by the Friends of Sefton. It commemorates John Sadler, his father Adam Sadler and Guy Green.

Adam (who fought with the Duke of Marlborough) was buried on 9th October 1765 followed by his wife Elizabeth on 15th May 1769. John (the potter) their son was buried on 14th December 1789, then his sons and a daughter in subsequent years. 'Roman' and 'Romanist' is written by some of the names in the register.

The War Memorial

This lies across the road from the church gate and incorporates stones from the old village cross [108] which had been built into a wall in Buckley Hill. Designed by Caröe and erected in 1920, it blew down three times and had to be shortened and have a steel rod inserted.

The Mill

The name Molyneux is derived from the French word for a mill and the Cross Moline might remind us of windmill sails. Sefton Mill used to lie to the east of the Church. The original mill was built in 1595 and had a four-centred doorway and chimney-piece which was probably of that date. Wheat, barley, oats, and rye were formerly grown, as well as potatoes; by the early nineteenth century cabbage was the chief crop.

[108]

The original Mill burnt down in 1941 and was excavated and covered before the new housing development went ahead. It was powered by the River Alt until the river was diverted along its present course.

Sefton Manor House

Part of the moat remains of the old Sefton Manor House in the field opposite the church, just beyond the War Memorial. This is a listed monument and on private land. Strangely, there is no known illustration extant. The house, which was huge, was partly dismantled about 1720 but the remains served as a farmhouse which was still standing in 1817. Cattle often drowned in its moat which was as wide as a canal, and it was originally surrounded by fine trees and an orchard.

To the south was a farmhouse, known as The Grange, which had retained some seventeenth-century details, and a barn of late sixteenth-century date.

St Helen's Well [109 and 110]

About three minutes walk along Lunt Road, the Well was held in former times to have healing properties and later used by visitors as a wishing-well. Continual ill-treatment of the Well and superstructure eventually led to its closure, but a few years ago it was restored although the water is inaccessible.

Now our short tour is over, you might like to wander around and revisit something of particular interest. This is a living church, so please show due reverence. I hope that you have enjoyed our perambulation.

1 Harleian MSS, No. 3764, f.8b.
2 Will signed 13th October 1553 (he died in 1558).
3 Dr Wall.
4 The use of this Chapel was one of the subjects of the long running feuds between the Molyneux and Blundells. Nicholas Blundell (died 1523) complained that Edward Molyneux (parson) among other 'wrongs and ingerys' had taken away his 'right of the church, that is to say of knely'g and tary'g in a chapel on ye north side of said church'.
5 Thomas Ashcroft, *A Brief Historical & Descriptive Account of Sefton Church, in the County of Lancaster*, (Liverpool, T. B. Johnson, 1819).
6 This Mrs Ann Molyneux of Liverpool was obviously a wealthy widow and well known to Squire Nicholas Blundell, but her precise heritage is unknown. It has been suggested that her husband was a wealthy grocer in Liverpool but he was still alive when she was described as 'a widow.'
7 Letter in Church archive.

No man, when he hath lighted a candle,
covereth it with a vessel . . . but setteth it
on a candlestick, that they which
enter in may see the light.

Luke 16–17

The reference numbers in the margins
refer to the Stations in the Guide Book

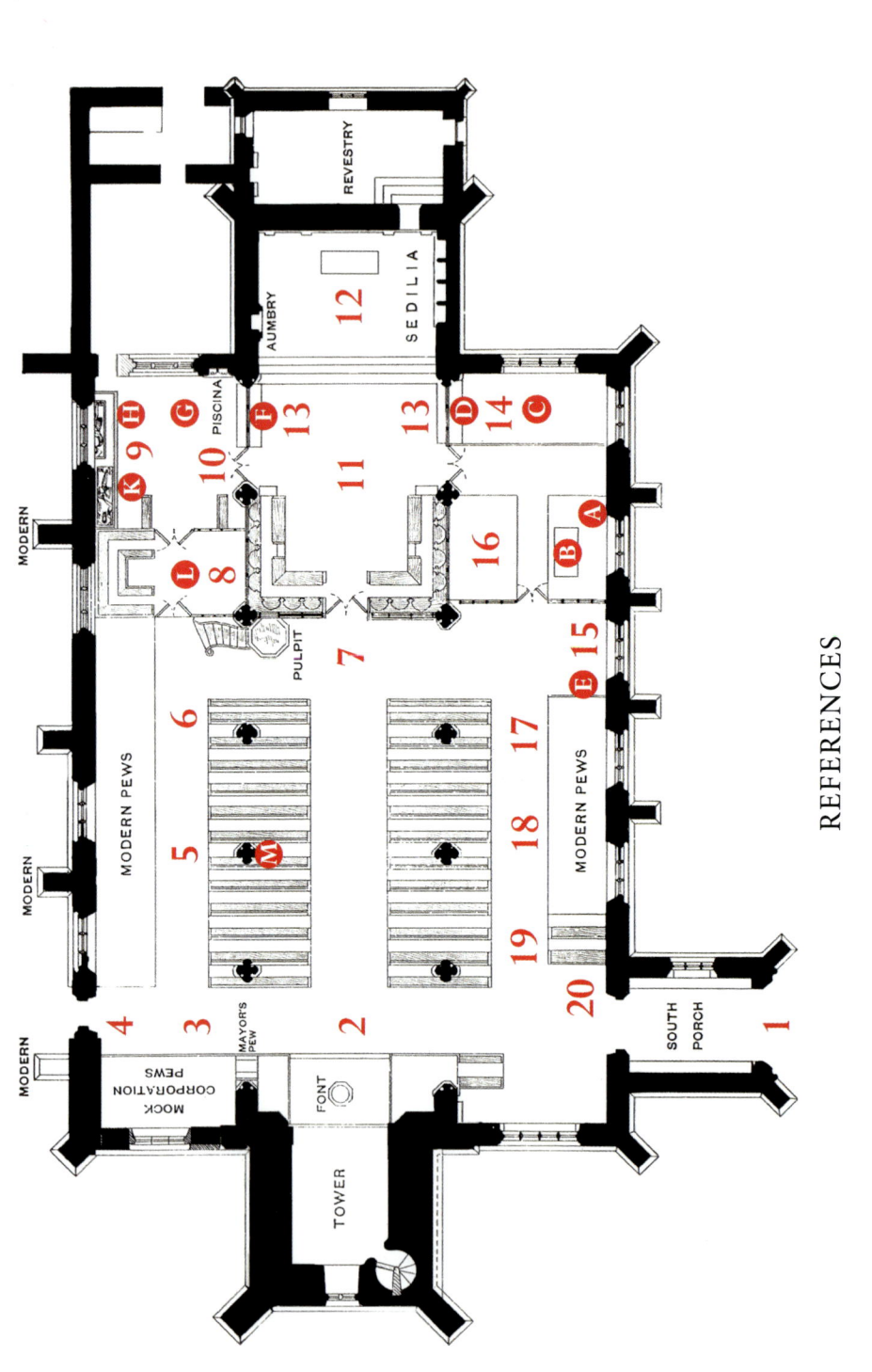

REFERENCES

A — Sefton Pew
B — Brass, Margaret Bulcley (1528)
C — { South east Chapel (formerly the Bulcley Chantry)
      { Sefton Monuments
D — Brass, Sir Rd. Molyneux (1558)

F — Johanna Molyneux (1439)
G — Lady Chapel (formerly the Molyneux Chantry)
H — Effigy, Sir Wm. Molyneux (1296–8)
K — Effigy (1325–40)
L — Blundell Chapel
M — Position of Pulpit before 1822

A noble witness to the piety and liberality of an age gone by

No doubt can exist that the church, and more especially the chancel, has been much despoiled. Its hangings have been torn down, its frescoes obliterated, its stained glass demolished, its brasses broken, its monuments defaced, the fabric itself in places injured; yet notwithstanding the handiwork of the iconoclast, and of the soldiers of the Commonwealth, it still remains a noble witness to the piety and liberality of an age gone by.

Rev G. W. Wall, Rector Read 7th March, 1895.
HISTORIC SOCIETY Lancashire and Cheshire.

Sefton Church seen from the air. *Photograph courtesy of Allan Lee McKay.*

Moveable Feast

The story of Sefton Church is complicated, not least because the Lords of the Manor of Sefton (Molyneux) reserved for themselves various areas of the church during different periods and two discrete local families (Blundell) used the same surname and occupied the same chapel.

The Molyneux Pew for instance is somewhat like a moveable feast: it started life in the north aisle near where Edward Molyneux founded his chantry, then migrated to the south aisle west of the screen, and later moved east of the screen to be renamed the Sefton Pew.

Most ancient churches have been rearranged at times but Sefton seems to have suffered more than its fair share. To add confusion, many earlier guide books have copied mistakes which in time have become truths. I have attempted to turn back the clock and show how the building has grown and developed under the influence of its benefactors and people. Not everything is known, or can be known but I hope that the facts will speak for themselves. I too will have erred, but please remember that forgiveness is divine.

Three Families

Three landowning families settled in the parish: Molyneux, the most powerful family in the region, Blundell of Ince and Blundell of Little Crosby. While a Crosby Blundell once married a Molyneux heiress, these two families were also involved in bitter disputes. The Molyneux family was determined to be next in line to the Stanley family, and on occasion behaved very badly to their neighbours, the Blundells of Little Crosby. The Molyneux family settled in Sefton and probably established the church next door. Here they later reserved a chapel in the new south aisle (nearest their house), and the Blundells, who became Lords of Little Crosby (a separate manor), gained rights to a chapel in the north aisle.

The Molyneux Connection

Guilliam Desmolines, the first Lord of Sefton, arrived in England with William of Normandy as the eighteenth man in the roll of noblemen listed at Battle Abbey.

William the Conqueror: the Hawk of Normandy.

The Conqueror gave all the lands between the Ribble and Mersey to Guilliam's friend, Roger Pictavensis, who in turn granted the Manors of Sefton, Thornton, and Cuerdale to Molyneux to hold by the Service of half a Knight's Fee. After the Reformation, the family established a Benedictine Mission in their manor at Cuerdale, near Preston.

The main Molyneux family lived at Sefton Hall opposite the church until 1702 when they removed to their lavishly rebuilt house and estate at Croxteth. It has often been said that this placed them closer to their interests in the booming town of Liverpool; in fact the reduction in distance is negligible. Croxteth certainly gave them the prospect of a much grander house and secluded park, but it also removed them from the prying eyes of the Church.

Sefton Manor House, with its moat of *c.*1372, served as a farmhouse from 1702 until 1817. After the Reformation, its Catholic Chapel operated as a Mass centre for the area until St Benet's Chapel across the fields in Netherton was built in the late 18th century. Many couples were married in Sefton Hall Chapel, some choosing to cross the road to Sefton Church to undergo another ceremony and have the marriage

The Molyneux Family gained the Constableship of Liverpool Castle in 1420.

legally entered in the registers. This was particularly true after the 1753 Hardwicke's Marriage Act which banned clandestine marriages. After 1836, Catholics were not obliged to marry in the Anglican Church.

The historic site was excavated in 1956–61 by the Archaeology Department of Merchant Taylor's School, which established the pre-existence of the Hall, a moat, a bowling green,

The Molyneux coat of arms.

chapel, tithe barn and Old Orchard House. Two large pieces of Roman–British pottery were also found there, which suggests a very ancient site of habitation. Sefton Hall was the largest house in the area and it is probable that Sefton Village's decline as a community started when the Molyneux Family moved to Croxteth and took with them many work opportunities. The family continued to maintain an association with Sefton until the 7th and last Earl, Hugh William Osbert, died in 1972 and the last Countess in 1980.

The Succession Crisis

In the mid-eighteenth century there was a problem in the Molyneux succession: in 1733 Richard (5th Viscount) died prematurely leaving only two daughters. He was succeeded by his brother Caryll (6th Viscount) who died leaving three sons.

Isabella, Countess of Sefton 1819
(formerly Isabella Stanhope).

The eldest, Richard, who was a Jesuit priest, succeeded as the 7th Viscount, followed by his brother William who was the 8th Viscount but unmarried. The youngest son, Thomas, had already died so Thomas' son, Charles William, succeeded in 1759 as 8th Viscount. After his father's premature death, Charles William had come under the influence of the establishment and was persuaded to convert to Anglicanism, which he did in 1769. In recognition of his conformity, the title of Viscount was upgraded in 1771 to that of Earl in the Peerage of Ireland. His son, William-Philip, the 2nd Earl had political leanings but failed to get himself elected to Parliament for Liverpool, although he was returned for Droitwich in 1816. In 1831 was created a baron of the United Kingdom as Lord Sefton of Croxteth.

20th Century

During the First World War, the family suffered the loss of its youngest son, the Hon. Cecil Richard Molyneux, who died aged 16 in the dreadful Battle of Jutland in 1916. When the 7th Earl died without issue in 1972, no heirs could be found and the estate at Croxteth was left for the enjoyment of the people of Liverpool. Had the Cecil Richard Molyneux survived the First World War and produced male heirs, the Earldom would probably be extant today.

Hugh William Osbert, 7th and last Earl of Sefton. *Image by Public Catalogue Foundation.*

Blundells of Crosby and Ince

The next two important families in the area confusingly share a name and are the Blundells of Crosby and the Blundells of Ince. Surnames only became strictly necessary with the introduction of poll taxes in the fourteenth century and it is important to separate these two distinct families. The Blundells of Crosby are descended from Osbert of Ainsdale who might have been of Saxon origin as his name is not Norman. The Blundells of Ince probably came over from Normandy in a second or later wave of settlers. By the second half of the twelfth century, Osbert of Ainsdale and Robert Blundell (of Ince) were both living.

Post-conquest integration was most important, and Osbert's family adopted their neighbours' Norman name of Blundell (which seems to indicate being blond-headed). Some centuries later the Ince family returned the compliment by adopting the Crosby family's coat of arms – which shows silver billets (or logs) against a black background. The crest of the Crosby Blundells is a demi-lion rampant holding in its paws a cross, while the Ince family has a squirrel sejant guardant, collared and holding a nut or (gold). The lion is a reference to the arms of the Villiers family which held the manor of Little Crosby before it was inherited by the Molyneux family. The Villiers had six lions rampant on their arms.

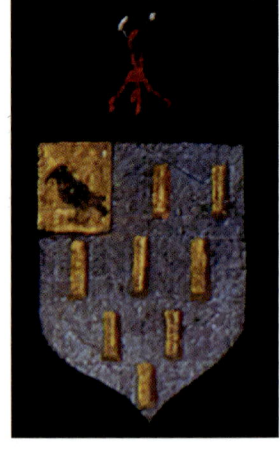

Version of Blundell of Ince arms. The motto: Quae Nocent, Docent (That which hurts, teaches).

Osbert's descendant, David Blundell, married Agnes Molyneux, and eventually the Blundells inherited the Manor of Little Crosby. Their descendants still live at Crosby Hall.

Robert Blundell had earlier been granted the adjacent Manor of Ince (*Ince* being an Old English word for *island*), which was later renamed Ince Blundell. Here the Blundells built their manor house and later a magnificent hall, chapel and miniature pantheon.

The Crosby Blundells ceased to use their chapel shortly before the Reformation, except for burials, but their namesakes, the Blundells of Ince, maintained an interest in the chapel. The Blundells of Ince, while harbouring Catholic priests at their Hall, sometimes put in minimal attendance at Sefton Church in order to avoid fines.

Only one Blundell of Ince (Robert Blundell of Ince 1575–1656/7, illustrated) actually conformed to the Church of England and he was lucky enough to make a fortune as a lawyer (Catholics were debarred from university, the law and civil offices). The Blundell Chapel became known as *The Squire of Ince's Pew*.

Robert Blundell of Ince
1575–1656/7.
A temporiser, he became a successful lawyer, amassing a fortune before returning to the Catholic faith. He was a close friend of the Blundells of Crosby.
Courtesy of Mark Blundell Esq.

The Blundell and Molyneux Dispute

The Crosby Blundells suffered a long-running assault by Dame Anne Molyneux and her son Edward (Rector of Sefton) which blighted neighbourly relationships for generations. Anne was the daughter of Sir Thomas Dutton of Dutton in Cheshire, and highly ambitious. Her husband, Sir William Molyneux was knighted in 1482 while fighting in the Scottish campaign, but died the following year leaving her a widow with a young family. The Victoria County History calls her, '*a vigilant guardian, bent on increasing the family possessions*'. Seeing the Blundells arriving at Sefton Church for Mass must have reminded the Molyneux family that Little Crosby Manor (always separate from Sefton Manor) was originally in its possession – until 1362. In a moment of Blundell weakness in 1514, Anne and Edward tried to seize the manor, which started a long and vicious assault which began with cattle rustling, then claiming a 'Fat Ox' belonging to a Blundell tenant as a 'mortuary' – a church due, and eventually driving the Blundells out of their manor houses in Crosby and Ditton. At the time, Lancashire was almost a lawless place, and the Molyneux family held sway over large parts of it, competing at this time with the upwardly socially mobile Stanley family. John Cokeson complained at the time that there was no justice because of '*the grate myght power, Kyne and Alie that the said Edward is of in that Cuntrey*'. The case rumbled on for years in and out of various courts, including the judicial Star Chamber. Cardinal Wolsey, the Lord Chancellor, knew only too well how justice in the provinces was more influenced by local powerful families than by ideas of fairness. Even when it was finally resolved in 1531 by Sir Thomas More, Edward was slow to implement the financial settlements and behaved badly. In 1535, just before his death, Edward founded his chantry, no doubt hoping that he would escape from the fires of purgatory early.

What is interesting for us is an extant letter which was drawn up by Nicholas Blundell. Among other things, it confirms that the Blundells did indeed have rights in a Chapel on the north side of Sefton Church – which Edward removed. We also learn about the domestic bliss formerly enjoyed by old Nicholas Blundell and his wife Margery and how Edward had split them up after 60 years of

Looking through the Blundell Chapel.

Charles Blundell Esq. of Ince on his favourite pony Davy with his attendant Mary Shaw.
Courtesy of Mark Blundell Esq.

happy marriage and 12 children. He says that they had been parted, '*contrarye to both yayre mynds god knows, whych have ben joinned to gedder three scaure years & have hade xii chylder togedder and never cold fynd fote noder with oder*'.

The last phrase is particularly touching when he says that they could never find fault with each other – in all those 60 years. Years later the Molyneux and the Crosby Blundell families were reconciled, having a common foe in the face of the Protestant Reformation.

Both Blundell families maintained Catholic missionary activities on their estates, and both were passionate Royalists, having their estates forfeited during the Civil War. Luckily, both were able to buy back their lands after the

46

Restoration with the help of both Catholic and Protestant friends. Both Blundell families produced some remarkable descendants, some of whom are mentioned in this book.

The estate of Charles Blundell of Ince (who died unmarried in 1837) passed to a relative, Thomas Weld (b. 1807), on the condition that he added the name Blundell to his own. The Weld family is an important family which descended from a Lord Mayor of London in 1608. Thomas' son Charles, after the death of his sons[1] during the First World War, left Ince Blundell to his two daughters for life, and then to the owner of Lulworth. The Hall and Garden were sold to an order of nuns, the Augustinian Canonesses and the remainder of the Estate sold to sitting tenants in the 1970s. The majestic Hall is now a convalescent home.

The Welds of Lulworth, who are descended from Joseph Weld (brother of Thomas), continue to live at the 12,000 acre Lulworth Castle Estate in south Dorset, while the Blundell Family of Little Crosby (after passing down the female line twice) still resides at Little Crosby where it has established an educational trust (CHET). In the late eighteenth century, the Crosby Blundells added the Manor of Crosby to that of Little Crosby.

Recusants in Sefton Parish: *No Hope of Reformation or Obedience in the Parts*

Having survived the pre-Reformation onslaught of the Molyneux family, little did the Blundells of Crosby know that their refusal to put the monarch before God would cause them 200 more years of misery. It is worth remembering the extraordinary practices the State pursued to enforce con-formity of religion and the heroic sacrifices made by the Blundells to resist them. While the Molyneuxes and Blundells of Ince occa-sionally and outwardly conformed to avoid crippling fines and demeaning imprison-ment, the Crosby Blundells always stood firm as 'stout recusants'.

On 31st January 1599, a weary Richard Vaughan, Bishop of Chester begged to disturb Secretary Cecil, and complained about the reception his envoys received in Lancashire, who had been 'so cruelly entreated'. They had probably been forced to eat their own war-

Pew end in the Blundell Chapel.

rants. We do know that a certain pursuivant called 'Crosse' 'was sore beaten' at Ollerton near Brindle on 10th August 1618.

The Bishop mentions Blundell, among others, '*who give countenance to all lewd practices*' and says that '*until they be bridled from above and brought in by a strong hand, there is no hope of reformation or obedience in these parts*'.

Of the twelve magistrates who had to take the oath of allegiance and supremacy, only three appear to be '*soundly affected in religion*'. Of all the knights, squires and minor gentry, only a tiny proportion were free from all suspicion. Many were recusants, and others had recusant wives but they themselves were '*comers to church but non-communicants*'.

'*Uncomformitie, obstinacie and disobedience*' – thirteen Years of Misery for the Blundells

A diary-style event list of the last thirteen years of Elizabeth I shows how Church and State dealt with the obstinate Blundells. On 11th June 1590 Richard Blundell was living with his wife Emilia (née Norris of Speke) and son William. The Earl of Derby sent men to search their house at Little Crosby – *for 'matters belonging to the Catholicke Religion'*. Mr Woodroffe (a seminary priest),

Death was a frequent visit to Sefton Parish.

Richard and his son William were taken to the New Parke (a home of the Earl) and examined by the Earl.

13th June 1590	Imprisoned in Chester Castle.
5th/6th August	Brought to Knowsley and examined by Bishop Chatterton of Chester.
Next day	Mr Woodroffe, Richard and William sent to gaol at Lancaster Castle.
19th March 1592	Richard dies. William allowed out on licence for one month to visit Crosby.
29th September	William allowed to go home.
20th/21st November	Parson John Nutter of Sefton with assistants arrest William and his wife and take them in custody to Sefton Parsonage for the night.
13th June 1590	William and wife taken to the New Parke to be examined by the Earl and the Bishop. Emilia is dismissed and sent home while William is sent to London.
8th December	William examined by Dr Whytgift, Archbishop of Canterbury at Croydon. William sent to the Gatehouse Prison in Westminster.
12th July 1595	William freed, upon bonds to appear again as necessary.
27th May 1598	Little Crosby searched by Sir Richard Molyneux and Parson John Nutter. William escapes while his wife is taken to Sefton to be examined, and sent home on bonds to appear at Chester before the Bishop.
31st May	Mrs Blundell, with others, taken to Chester Castle. While in prison, the old indictment of entertaining a seminary priest from 1590 reappears, and William is summoned to appear at the County Court in Lancaster. He does not show, and spends nine months as an outlaw hiding out in various country houses.

Emilia is let out on bonds, and joins her husband in Wrexham where William's brother-in-law (named Banister) lives. Emilia becomes pregnant and returns to her own family – the Norrises of Speke. William goes to another Banister house – this time in Wemys.

He then decides to go to London to seek a pardon, but after five weeks with no luck, moves to Staffordshire and changes his name.

He is later joined by his wife and for the next two years they live in six places.

24th March 1603 Queen Elizabeth dies. The terror is over (momentarily) and he is granted from the new King James 'a free and large pardon' for a few shillings.

All hära Cyrice – the *Harkirke*.

While it was relatively easy for recusants to receive the sacraments in Sefton Parish, a government plot was hatched to refuse them burial in their parish churches. Just before Christmas in 1610, William Blundell heard about the death of a local woman who was refused burial at Sefton. Her relatives dug a shallow grave outside the churchyard wall near the highway, but soon horses' hooves disturbed her body, and wandering swine consumed part of it.

Following his own catechism's teaching on the last Corporal Work of Mercy – *burying the dead* – he decided to enclose a piece of ground on his estate which of old was called the *Harkirke*. In old Scandinavian, the name signified '*an old hoary church*'. The day after its completion, a hoard of buried silver coins from the age of Catholic Saxon kings was found by a fourteen-year-old local boy, Thomas Ryse, who was driving cattle across the area. William felt that he was a modern Tobias, fearing God more than the king and being re-warded. He made a careful drawing of some of them. Although a pyx was made out of some of the silver, most of them were sent to Wales for safe-keeping at a time of war, and there sadly lost.

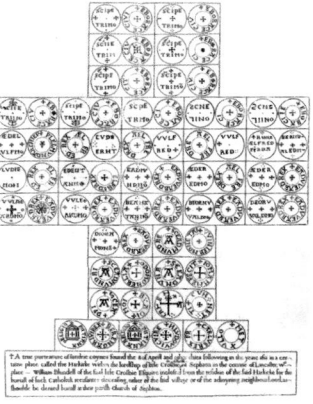

Many people were refused burial at that time, and it was common to make graves in gardens, fields and hedgerows. The first Harkirke burial took place on 7th April 1611 when William Mathewson was refused burial at Sefton. Most of the interments up to about 1620 were made after being refused elsewhere. Charite Melling, daughter of Richard Melling of Melling was refused at Melling Chapel and so was buried in the Harkirke in 1614. John Synett, was buried in 1613 after being excommunicated by the Bishop of Chester and refused burial

Engraving of the some of the old English coins found at the Harkirk in 1611.

at Liverpool. James Whitmore, from Thurstaston on the Wirral was buried in 1623 and John Nicholasson of Much Crosby was buried in 1627 after 'being somewhat overseene wth drink (as it was thought)' and 'drowned in a pitte'.

Fortunately the Blundells kept a detailed register of burials and we still have a drawing of some of the coins (illustrated).

For his efforts, William Blundell was brought before the notorious Star Chamber and fined an astonishing £2,300. The cemetery was later desecrated by the king's soldiers who levelled most of the stones, although thankfully, they did not disturb the burials.

Please note that numbers refer to stations in the Guide Book section.

1 WHO WAS ST HELEN?

In over two thousand years of Christian history, there are inevitably going to be many saints sharing the same Christian name. In England, a popular legend told that Helena was the daughter of the King of Britain, Cole of Colchester – the familiar 'Old King Cole', who allied himself with Constantius and brokered peace between Britain and Rome. There was certainly a cult around St Helen as there were at least twenty-five holy wells dedicated to her.

In reality, she is likely to be the Helena who was the mother of Constantine the Great who was born in the middle of the third century and died about 330. She was of humble birth and St Ambrose called her a *stabularia*,[2] or inn-keeper. Incredibly she married Constantius, Co-Regent of the West, who later deserted her.

Her son Constantine, however, succeeded his father, and summoned his mother to the Imperial Court, as well as converting her to Christianity. She was honoured, and coins were even struck bearing her profile. Direct evidence of her piety is attested by Eusebius (Bishop of Caesarea) (Vita Constantini,

The south porch (*c.*1500).

III, xivii): '*She became under his influence such a devout servant of God, that one might believe her to have been from her very childhood a disciple of the Redeemer of mankind*'.[3]

Churches were erected by her in Rome and Trier (both Imperial cities) and even in advanced years she took a trip to Palestine, building a church in Bethlehem and another near the Mount of Olives near Jerusalem. There are abundant stories of her piety, and her care for individuals as well as whole communities.

In Jerusalem, she discovered the pagan temple built over the Holy Sepulchre and ordered it to be torn down. During excavations, it is said that she discovered three crosses, but being pragmatic and a sceptic, she found a woman who was close to death and invited her to touch the first and the second cross. Nothing happened – her state did not change. On touching the third cross, the woman suddenly made a total recovery. Helena declared this to be the true cross, the *Santa Croce*. It is said that she also found the nails of the crucifixion. Constantine ordered the building of the Church of the Holy Sepulchre on the site, and to protect him, she later had a piece of the cross placed in his helmet and another in the bridle of his horse.

She brought large pieces of the cross to Rome where her memory is best preserved at the Church of S. Croce in Gerusalemme, near which formerly stood the *Thermae Helenianae* and the *Palatium Sessorium*. It is likely that she lived at the Lateran nearby, as two inscriptions dedicated to Helen were found there. Helen might have proposed the building of the basilica dedicated to the True Cross on the site of her house. Soil from Golgotha was allegedly brought to Rome and spread over the Vatican Gardens, to unite Christ's blood symbolically with the blood of the early Christian martyrs in Rome who perished under Nero.

She is also credited with starting the large population of cats in Cyprus, in order to rid a monastery of snakes.

Helen has also been blamed for introducing idolatry into the Church by popularising the idea of relics, but this issue was settled at the Second Council of Nicaea, although it erupted again during the Protestant Reformation.

At Sefton, there is a nearby Well dedicated to St Helen, and there is a mediaeval Church of St Helen at Garstang (Kirkland). The original Chapel at St Helens was also dedicated to St Elyn (first extant record 1552), as was that at Tarleton.

In Sefton Church there is a large number of pew ends carved with the implements of the passion and maybe this is a link to St Helen's finding of the true cross and nails. The early twentieth-century statue above the church porch shows St Helen crowned, holding the Cross.

St Helen, carrying the true cross, from the Audley window.

Twentieth-century statue of St Helen, above the porch.

2 BELLS

1. Treble WE COMMEMORATE THE VICTORY & VICTORS 1945 GIVEN IN MEMORY OF MY DEVOTED WIFE ELIZABETH PARTRIDGE BY THOMAS PARTRIDGE
PRAISE MY SOUL THE KING OF HEAVEN TAYLOR 1946

2. WE COMMEMORATE THE VICTORY & VICTORS 1945 GIVEN BY PARISH SUBSCRIPTION W. W. LONGFORD D. D. RECTOR
S. S. EASTWOOD E. M. HOUGHTON CHURCH WARDENS PRAISE HIM IN THE HIGHEST

3. WILLM DOBSON FOUNDER.
W. ECCLESTON AND R. ROSE
CH WDNS 1815

Engraved on the crown:
RICHARD RAINSHAW ROTHWELL
RECTOR. THO: IOHNSON CURATE
PETER BLACKBURN CHRISTOPHER
RICHMOND CHURCHWARDENS
ELECT

Dedication of the two new bells to commemorate the end of the Second World War.

4. OUR VOICES SHALL WITH JOYFUL SOUND MAKE HILLS AND VALLEYS ECHO ROUND

Engraved on the crown:
RICHARD RAINSHAW ROTHWELL RECTOR. THO: IOHNSON CURATE PETER BLACKBURN CHRISTOPHER RICHMOND CHURCHWARDENS 1815

5. GOD BLES THE FOVNDER HEAROF 1601

6. Nos sumus constructi ad Lavdvm Domini 1601 (translated as: *We are cast to the praise of the Lord*)

7. Hec Campana Beata Trinitate Sacea Fiat (translated as: *May this bell be blessed by the Holy Trinity*)

On Waist:
Circular Stamp of Henry Oldfield

8. Hec Campana Beata Trinitate Sacea Fiat

On Waist:
Circular Stamp of Henry Oldfield

3 THE MOCK CORPORATION OF SEFTON

In the eighteenth century, Liverpool experienced a boom in its business and wealth, all derived from shipping. Its fine, broad streets were paved with imagined gold and its Moot Hall was rebuilt as a grand Mansion House (now the Town Hall) to rival any in Europe, which it still does.

James Williamson, the Recorder of Sefton Corporation.

A group of moneyed gentlemen decided to form a Sunday social club where they could escape from their tiring labours in the hot, seething town.

Mock Corporations seem to derive from an idea that the ancient king-given rights of the people had been usurped by subsequent legislation. Some were overtly political, and often Jacobite at a time of civil unrest about the Succession. At Sefton, they drew their authority from an imagined Charter from William the Conqueror bestowed in 1014 (*sic*), although the like-minded gentlemen seemed merely to enjoy the company of each other. Of course there was plenty of drinking (at least one bottle of wine each) and they ate copiously, and usually attended the established church in specially reserved pews.

Why they settled on Sefton Village is anyone's guess. The locality had been renowned in previous centuries for its bowling clubs and leisure activities so maybe there was a distant memory of that. It was just far enough away from the town, yet not too far, and it enjoyed bracing sea air in a rural setting. Another likely reason is its convenience for travel on horseback. Inland routes from Liverpool are mostly uphill, and in those days, on poor bridle paths passing areas of habitation. The route to Sefton, however, was along the sandy foreshore, passing hardly anyone or anything. Only the last run through Litherland was across country. This would be convenient, especially for return journeys, with riders suffering from various states of inebriation: the horses probably knew their own way home. The opening of the canal on 1st January 1774 enabled members to walk to their winter retreat at the home of Thomas Halliwell (Bootle Coffee House, now where Merton Road crosses the canal).

Pewter plate once used by the Mock Corporation.

Only one instance of arranged transport is mentioned – on 1st January 1774 when 'a coach and one pair of Horses, (was) to come to Bootle at four o'clock in the Afternoon'.

We are not sure when the Corporation was founded but the first recorded meeting was held on 15th October 1753, probably at Sefton for the purposes of choosing a Mayor (Samuel Smith). It can hardly have been the first meeting as there was already a Mayor, Bailiff, Aldermen and twenty-three burgesses appointed. Among those who voted was John Delaney, inn-holder and landlord of the Sefton Inn. There is also a curious reference to something even earlier in an entry of 1764 which refers to the '*Oath of a Common Council Man of Sephton as extracted from an old Record much defaced*', although the eighteen Common Councillors appended to this oath appear in the same book which only starts in 1753.

The second and third meetings recorded in 'Sephton Records' were held at Baxters (sometimes a public house) in Down Litherland (Great Crosby marsh, in modern-day Seaforth):

'11th November, 1753. At a meeting held at Phillip Syers alias Baxter Bor. in Order to fill up the vacant offices',

and, 'December 21st, 1753. A council being held at Baxter Borough'.

The last mention of Baxters in the minutes was on 11 November 1764, perhaps because Syers ceased to be an innkeeper.

Caroe's records end in 1797, although the last minutes imply that meetings were going to continue and members were actually enrolled in a small book until the

Touch mark on pewter dish from the Corporation service.

last entry on 27th May 1829. After 1772, winter meetings took place at the Coffee House in Bootle – at that time a fashionable seaside village. At both Sefton and Bootle, they mimicked the Corporation of Liverpool by having a Mayor and full council as well as their own Mansion Houses (the Inns), council chambers and full regalia. At Sefton they were blessed by having 'The Cathedrall' – something which even Liverpool lacked.

Another early record of the Corporation's existence was a mace, engraved 'The gift of F. Cust, Esq., 1764'. On the side opposite to the name was the representation of a wild boar with the motto underneath 'Vivimus'. It might have originally read 'Dum vivimus vivamus' (*While we live, let us live*) (or even 'Dum vivimus bibamus' (*While we live, let us drink*) but the characters had become obliterated.

Sometimes members behaved as if they were the real Corporation of Liverpool. They inspected the markets for measures and quality, they put unruly military men in the Bridewell, and even hijacked a Grand Ball in Liverpool. On Sunday 22nd March 1789 they announced:

'A Ball at the Corporation's expense was moved by the Mayor . . . to be given in the 16th of next month in the Exchange to the Ladies and Gentlemen of the Borough'.

'Sefton Abbey' – oil painting by John Innes Herdman 1875. Oil on canvas.
Courtesy of E. J. Crighton.

In reality, this was a grand affair to be provided by Liverpool Town Council for its own citizens of quality. Despite this comic rivalry, members seemed to enjoy good relations with their counterparts in Liverpool, as when on Christmas Day 1791, several Sefton Burgesses dined at the Mayor's House in Liverpool.

The Mayor-making ceremony always took place on 18th October, St Luke's Day (the same day as in Liverpool), and in addition there was a Town Clerk, bailiffs, a Recorder and many other officers. New members were required to take an oath and drink on the mace – wine or sometimes beer had to be quaffed directly from the trumpet of the regalia. If anyone refused the particular office given to them, they were soon expelled. Suffice to say that those who initially declined a post, swiftly changed their minds.

There were many Officers' posts available. Apart from the mundane postings such as *Surveyors*, *Master of the Fox Hounds* and *Poet Laureate*, there were *Ambassadors to foreign climes*, *An American Consul*, and a *Translator of Oriental Languages*. There was also a noticeable African influence, with *An African Committee Man*, *A Governor of the Tantum Quarry* (Gold Coast) *and A Prince of Annamaboe* (Ghana). The original 'Prince of Annamaboe' was a black celebrity, the son of a wealthy Ghanaian and African Slave trader. On a lighter note, there was an *Inspector of the Coney Warren* (rabbits), a *Groom of the Bed Chamber*, a *Hosier General*, *Window Peeper*, and an *Overseer of the Bastard Children*. Among the most bizarre descriptions given to members are Robert Parry, *tabellion (scrivener) and notary public;* John Slater, *poison seller;* John Luthner, *outlaw;* Captain Robert Moore, *Lonsdale Local Militia, of everywhere;* Pierce Somerset Butler, *Ireland, man of pleasure;* Th. G. Duarte, *Portuguese, a man of ships.*

Modern-day Blue Coat children at Sefton Church.

Sefton Church became the centrepiece of the Corporation's devotions, especially on St Luke's Day when the Mayor would process in state, accompanied by maces and silver oars. The Sunday preceding St Luke's Day was called *Waiting Sunday*, perhaps waiting for St Luke's Day, although in 1790 they inexplicably had two 'Waiting Sundays' – one before and one after. It was on this day that the boys from the Blue Coat Hospital in Liverpool accompanied the Mayor to church. How they got there is unexplained, as the packet boat on the canal did not sail on Sundays. Maybe they arranged a special sailing or arrived in horse-drawn wagons along the shore. Several Burgesses were also Trustees of the Hospital which relied totally on charity donations, so their visit to Sefton would put the Blue Coat foremost in the minds of many of its leading citizens. Oddly, no actual collections ever seem to have been taken on these occasions. On one Waiting Sunday, the weather was so inclement that the Mayor-elect and bailiffs did not attend, but the boys somehow managed to arrive and went to church with their masters instead, no doubt enjoying the relative freedom of the outing.

Some Burgesses went to church twice but usually only the evening service was attended. Not all were disposed to piety, though, and often wagers were placed on the length of sermons, while others slept off the effects of their over-indulgence.

The signal to attend was *the great bell at the Corporation Church ... ceasing to toll* (17th June 1792). On one Sunday, a Burgess decided to stay in the Council Chamber while others went to the River Alt to catch the *'Scaly Tribes'*, producing sixteen fish for a snack after dinner. One Burgess, called Mr Bright, claimed in 1791 that he had not been to church in eleven years, but went that day to visit a friend instead. Once in 1789, a burgess *'came into the Church just in time for the "Gloria Patria"'*.

The north door, used for funerals in the north churchyard and possibly by the Mock Corporation members.

A typical timetable might be Dinner at 1.30pm in winter or 2.00pm in summer, Service about 5pm, and retirement at 7pm.

The victuals usually consisted of something like *'a boiled cod-fish, a couple of boil'd fowls, a roasted shoulder of mutton, a roasted spare rib of pork, a plum pudding, minc'd pyes, toasted cheese and some pretty tippling ale'*. On Sunday 26th July 1789, on the occasion of St James' Day Fair, the burgesses treated themselves to Westphalia Ham and Best London Particular Madeira while on 30th May they ended their dinner which included a boiled *'Calve's Head'* and *'Calve's Brains and Red Rage'* with Newborough cheese and a *'Bottle of good old wine vintage M:D:C:L:X:'* which was probably port produced in 1660.

The entry for 9th July 1797 presents a picture of contentment. The Burgesses,

> *Dined together, & after the Congregation had retired from Church, drank their Wine & smoaked their Pipes in the Corporation Alcove, & concluded the Evening with their accustomed harmony.*

Reverse of pewter plate.

Rare pen and ink drawing of Skating on Sefton Meadows. Early nineteenth century.
Courtesy of Dilly and Maurice Hayman.

Drinking wine was central to their activities – and all opportunities for a toast – loyal or otherwise – were rarely missed. As such, the Office of Vintner was most important. On 16th July 1797 there were eleven people present but only ten bottles of wine. This constituted serious failure of duty and the Vintner was dismissed for *his very great neglect.* The Corporation was forced to send an envoy to Mrs Unsworth at Maghull Manor House who kindly filled the void.

Too much wine probably proved the undoing of some members on their way home. On 26th October 1788, the first meeting at Bootle that season, The Recorder and Burgess Dunn were walking home along the canal path when Dunn *involuntarily but yet of his own accord and without any impulse ab extra, walked into the Canal where he was exposed to a most copious ablution.*

It was ordered that the Canal bank be surveyed to prevent *a similar accident in future, whereby the life of a worthy Burgess prone to Liquor might be endangered.* (9th November 1788).

It might have been more prudent to moderate their drinking habits, yet alcohol was part of the ritual. On Sunday 10th July 1791 they noted that Burgess Robert Lunt was at Church '*in a most drunken situation, to the small disgrace of the Corporation, and (what is of infinitely more consequence) our Holy Religion'.* Ironically, the very next paragraph congratulates a new Burgess for drinking a mace full of Porter, '*in a masterful style'.* On an earlier occasion in 1789 we hear of a new Burgess who '*swallowed the oath in Grog with a most amazing appetite'.*

When on 13th August 1797 only two Burgesses turned up, they felt obliged to support the '*Honor of the Corporation by taking their bottle, a Dinner and Smack'.*

Wine was also a useful fine, for when the Master of Music's dog appeared in the room on 8th October 1797, the Burgess was fined '*one bottle of wine'.*

In 1791 it was reported that *a Great Big Hole* had appeared on the shore which caused Burgess Laval's Palfrey to start and he '*lost the cover lid of his peri cranium'.* There was more drink trouble on 30th April 1797 when it was noted that members dined, '*comfortably ... and enjoyed the Corporation Wine very much'.* In the next paragraph, however, we are told that on the previous Sunday, some Burgesses, '*either from their want of knowledge of horsemanship or having taken too large draughts of the Corporation Wine*' were '*found seperated* (sic) *from their steeds on the Shore*'. The Bellman was so seriously injured that the Parish Cart had to be launched to take him home. And we can only speculate why, on 14th January 1792, the Mayor had been subjected to an '*intemperate plunge at the Whale Fishery at Murphy's*'.

Sefton Church in winter by J. A. Tanner.
Courtesy of Arthur and Pam Wright.

The steeple of Sefton Church was of interest to the Corporation, partly one suspects, from a degree of self-preservation as their commodious pews and nearby Council Chamber lay beneath its shadow. Mr James Grundy was ordered to survey it and duly reported on 14th September 1788:

'*The steeple did not stand quite so stiff and firm as it should do, and that the Cock appeared . . . to be much out of order and not capable of giving so much satisfaction as might be expected in its accustomed veerings and motions.*

It was unanimously ordered that ye steeple be immediately pulled down and rebuilt in a tight, stiff, staunch, and strong manner, so as in future to give no cause of Complaint to any Freeman or his wife, and that the Cock be neatly gilt and put into the best trim possible for performing its operations in future'.

Carved stone head
on a gatepost in Sefton Park
(South Liverpool)

This was a wise operation, as in 1802, after a hurricane when the tide rose an extra six feet, the spire lost its top five feet.

All, however, was not so sweet and it is inevitable that disputes arose. On 19th July 1789, the Town Clerk ordered the Accountant General to inspect the Treasurer's Accounts, and the following week, the Treasurer, Henry Newsham Esq was removed from his Office. Apparently he had embezzled a large sum of money which he had extracted from tradesmen working for the Corporation, on the promise of discount.

A much sadder expulsion took place on 8th April 1792 when Mr James Williamson (illustrated on page 53), the eminent Recorder left the Corporation, and its members even refused to allow him to resign honourably. We do not know his grave offence but it seems to be connected with a wager he had made on 19th February for an enormous sum of 50 guineas. He had arranged to drink with the Mayor, and bet that the Mayor would get drunk first. We do not know the outcome of the drinking competition – maybe independent observers deemed that he had lost when he claimed he had won. It was with the greatest sadness that he had to be expelled.

The Age of Enlightenment did not extend to all peoples of the planet. Shipping relied on cargo, human or otherwise, and the Corporation was firmly against any interference in their trade. They did not see any contradiction between their personal faith and their business matters.

Liverpool, like Bristol and London, was strongly in favour of the slave trade and in 1784, 11,000 of its total population of 41,000 signed the petition against Sir William Dolben's Bill in parliament to limit the number of slaves on each ship.

In 1789, the Corporation vigorously opposed this tightening of the regulations, and sent two members, Alderman Newsham and Burgess Wharton to London to oppose any changes. They were further resolved to send '15 *spirited resolutions*' (passed in Liverpool) to the House of Commons, and named the Chief Antagonist the '*Fanatic Wilberforce*'. On 20th February 1791, they rejoiced in a huge Sail of 200 Vessels which had left Liverpool on one day, although Liverpool historians Gore and Baines both state the figure as 350. Whatever the number, it must have been a magnificent sight.

A rare eighteenth-century view of the old Cust House, with the castle in the background.

Caröe draws our attention to an incident at the Theatre Royal in Liverpool when the celebrated actor George Frederick Cooke, partially intoxicated, was hissed at by the audience. He lurched forward as if to apologise, but instead exuded these memorable lines:

'*I despise you. There is not a brick in your nasty town but is cemented by the blood of the suffering African*'. Then he beat a hasty retreat to save his own life.

The Corporation was always on the lookout for social advantages, so when the news came through that a celebrated Irish giant was in the Borough, they were keen to sign him up, especially as he was a direct descendant of Brian Boru (*c.* 941–23 April 1014), King of Ireland.

Patrick Cotter, born in 1761, was an impressive 8ft. 7ins. and was said to be travelling in a post chaise. A deputation consisting of the Recorder armed with his silver oar and Burgess Grundy waving the Great Seal, was dispatched to find him and grant him the Freedom of the Borough. Imagine their disappointment when they caught up with him, but he declined the honour.

Other visitors were successfully drawn to the Corporation as on Sunday 18th June 1797 when '*a strange party of Psalm Singers visited the Mansion House after the Divine Service, & their Band played the favourite Air of God Save the King*'.

As the surviving Minutes draw to a close at the end of the summer of 1797, business in Sefton went on as usual. New Burgesses appeared and quaffed the Oath, the British Fleet was toasted for its glorious defeat of the Dutch Navy and the Blue Coat boys attended Church on Waiting Sunday. There is no indication of a disaster looming despite a slight (but not unusual) hint of fantasy: on 22nd October 1797 Thomas Woodward Esq was elected Mayor to serve the following year, with a massive majority of 222 votes and '*sworn into Office, and chaired amongst the acclamations of Thousands of Spec-*

A noble slave in chains
– on Nelson's monument
in Liverpool.

tators'. It is hard to imagine that the Corporation could draw such a gathering.

A Lady Patroness was chosen and Officers sworn, as usual. The final minutes for that summer season in Sefton order that the Head Constable should remove the Regalia and records etc. to Bootle, '*under a strong guard*' in preparation for the first winter meeting. Did they ever arrive? Was he ambushed, as fragments of a sword hilt were found in a ditch at Sefton in the later nineteenth century. As already noted, however, some business continued until at least 1829 when the last recorded member was admitted, although 'dead' was written against most of the preceding entries.

Most of the regalia was sold for £41 in 1887 by the Landlord of the *Punch Bowl* to the *Bear's Paw* Restaurant in Liverpool from which it found its way onto display in the Liverpool Museum. Here it remained, much admired by the public, until it was destroyed by enemy action in World War II. Thanks to Eveline B. Saxton who read a paper on the Early Records to the Historic Society of Lancashire and Cheshire on 18th November 1948, we have a list of items destroyed:

Dish and Minute Book with a message 'To the Loyal and Peaceable Inhabitants of Liverpool' at a time of strife in France. 1795.

1 A large mace of tin, silvered and gilded. Round the body were four panels and rosettes alternately; on the first panel was painted the inscription: *The gift of F. Cust, Esq. A.Dom. 1764*; on the second, a turtle; on the third below an obliterated picture is *VIVIMUS*; and on the fourth a rat or pig running.

2–3 Two small maces of tin, gilded and painted; on one of them the top piece (consisting of crown, fleur-de-lys, etc.) is removable, revealing a cup-shaped cavity for drinking purposes. It was from this mace that all new members drank when taking the oath of membership.

4 Large wooden mace, gilt, surmounted with brass cross.

5 Iron sword in a wooden case, the handle of brass, studded with white paste: one arm missing.

6 Iron sword, the pommel and guard gilt; handle and sheath covered with red plush with gilt bands.

7 Oar of tin, gilded and painted with a turtle on one side and a fish on the other.

(As no other oar is mentioned in the minutes, this seems to be the *silver* oar referred to on the 5 November 1786: *Ordered that the Silver Oar presented to this Borough by the late much respected John Brownwell, Esqre., Lieut. of the Seraphis in the memorable action with Paul Jones in the late War, be repaired, & thereon be inscribed: 'The Gift of John Brownwell, Esqre, to the Boro' & Corporation of Sephton'*).

The Corporation was called upon in October 1787 to pay for this Oar, and it was agreed to rescind the above Order.

8–10 Two black gowns, with velvet and silk (Bailiff) facings, and a felt hat, very much moth-eaten.

11–12 Two minute books of the 'Corporation of Sephton', for the years 1771–1786 and 1786–1797.

13 Book containing the forms of 'Oath on Taking Office, Freeman's Oath', etc., as well as a list of the members of Mock Corporation. Cash account book of the Corporation from 1754 to 1829.

15 A Copy of the Proceedings of the General United Society for supplying the British Troops upon the Continent with extra clothing, etc. London, 1798. (Presented to the Sephton Society at Liverpool.) The Sephton Society contributed £105, in addition to 500 shirts.

16–18 Along with the above objects, though probably not part of the regalia, was a Scottish claymore, a metal stand, and an estate account book.

re-creation of the Mock Corporation, 2008 to celebrate Liverpool as European Capital of Culture.
ographs courtesy of Allan Lee McKay.

Luckily, the main records (1771–1797) had been copied and published by Caröe in 1893 before the originals were destroyed. Two years after the end of World War II, something extraordinary happened: an original handwritten book called 'Sephton Records' was donated to the Liverpool Public Library which covered the period from 18th October 1753 to 19th June 1796. This volume is of immense value as it revealed details of the earliest meetings and members. We can also still view the Corporation Pew in 'The Cathedrall' at Sefton and even better, we can still enjoy their antics in our own imaginations.

As the Sefton Corporation faded away, perhaps another arose in its stead. We are informed by Richard Brooke FSA (author of *Liverpool As It Was 1775–1800*) that in the early nineteenth century, there was a Mock Corporation in Liverpool called 'The Mayor and Corporation of Asses' Green', a name derived from a piece of unenclosed land between Roscoe Street and Rodney Street, close to St Luke's Church (founded 1811). It consisted of working men and met annually on St Luke's Day, 18th October (the same civic day as in Sefton and Liverpool) at Page's Tavern in Roscoe Street. The ceremony of Chairing a Mayor took place at nightfall. He was then carried in procession attended by drums and fifes, with colours and occasional torches, and accompanied by a considerable crowd. When the procession reached a point about halfway between Leece Street and Knight Street, the populace lustily sang 'God Save the King'. It ceased to exist about 1830.

'The Clubbists'. An early nineteenth-century view by David Wilkie.

3 BENEFACTORS' BOARD

This charming old painted board was placed here in 1714 on the instructions of Nicholas Blundell and Thomas Syer, Church Wardens. It is reminiscent of a period looking-glass frame and the painting is quite naïve.

1714
NICH.BLUNDELL Esq.
THO. SYER. CROSBY MAGNA
CHURCH WARDENS
A True Life of Such Who have been so,
Charitable, as to Bestow Any Thing Towards,
The Better Maintenance of the Poore of
This, our Parish of Sefton, or Any Good use.

Below is a list, including large bequests of £12 from Ralf Low of Little Crosby (1713), £10 from Rev Mr Richmond (1713), a silver flagon to the value of £17 10s from Mrs Jackson (1715), £16 from Anthony Copple of Ford (1732), £40 (1732) from Mrs Anne Molyneux of Liverpool to buy a silver chalice and make the altarpiece (reredos), as well as gifts from the retiring Church Wardens Syer and Blundell of 10s and £5 respectively (1715).

Henry Blundell of Ince
Henry Blundell sits upon an antique chair directing attention to the object of Charity with his right hand and with his left hand, raising Genius from obscurity.

O blest with all that life to man endears!
Belov'd, repected, crown'd with length of years!
Form'd to enjoy what taste could e'er impart
From scenes of nature, or from works of art;
Works, that 'ere while in polish'd Athens known,
Yet live in lasting brass, or breathing stone.
But these no more now charm his cultur'd eye,
Frail flowers of earth, that only smile and die.
Tis CHARITY survives the general doom
Springs with perennial growth and triumphs o'er the Tomb.

William Roscoe

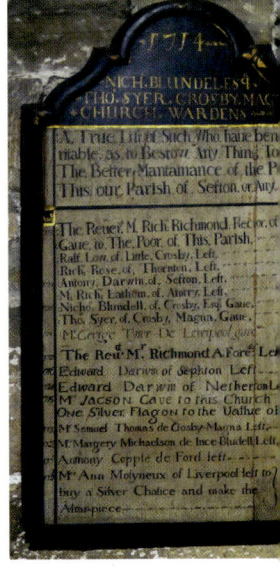

Nicholas Blundell's table of benefactors 1714.
He got the idea from seeing a similar one
in St Nicholas' Church, Liverpool.

Blundell Hall today – with its miniature pantheon.　　Classical garden temple at Ince Blundell Hall.

William Roscoe.
Poet, philanthropist and
MP for Liverpool. 1813.

4　CHILD PEARSON AND ZACHARIAS WINDOW

The window is divided into three lights.

West:
St Oswald, K.M. †
Badge of the South Lancashire Prince of Wales Volunteers
Lieutenant-Colonel John H Child Pearson DSO
South Lancashire Regiment
Killed in Normandy
August 1944

Centre:
St George, Martyr †
In Proud Memory of Two Friends who served England with Devotion

East:
St Edmund K.M. †
Badge of the Lancashire Fusiliers
Major John Paul Zacharias
Lancashire Fusiliers & Royal Tank Regiment
Killed in Action in Italy
September 1944

The two men commemorated in the window were childhood friends, living in the same road, being the same age and from the same social background. They were both married in Sefton Church and both were killed in active combat – in France and Italy.

Lieut Col John Harold Child Pearson DSO

John was the only son of Charles Child Pearson CBE and his wife, of Blundellsands. Educated at Uppingham and Sandhurst, he served in India before the war. He married Maud Wem Rowland of Blundellsands at Sefton Church on 5th January 1939. They had one son, Michael.

He landed in France on D-Day 6th June 1944.

John Harold and his unit were trying to force a river crossing before the objective, Mount Pincon, could be taken. Every attempt to take the bridge had been met with enemy fire. Col Pearson, determined to take the bridge, and wearing the traditional emblem of a 'red rose', strode down the middle of the road

Memorial window to
John H. Child Pearson and
John Paul Zacharias, featuring
SS Oswald, George and Edmund.

Exterior view of the war
memorial window.

with his stick and across the bridge, steadying his men and urging them forward. They took the bridge but a little beyond it he was mortally wounded.

Died 7th August 1944. Buried in the Tilly-sur-Seulles War Cemetery, Calvados, France (Ref. VI CI).

Major John Paul Zacharias

John Paul was the son of Frederick Albert Paul and Gladys Zacharias of Blundellsands and educated at Marlborough College. After leaving school he joined his father's firm of Cotton Merchants in Liverpool. He played both golf and rugby at the highest amateur levels – for England and Lancashire, and was a member of Formby GC and Waterloo RUFC. He married his American wife, Audrey Amsdale, at Sefton Church on 7th July 1937 and had one son John Dale who was three when his father died.

Major Fearnley, who served with John Paul Zacharias, described his new Commander of 'B' Squadron in an unpublished memoire as follows:

> *'Fresh out from England – John Zacharias – was a remarkable man, a "big" man in every sense of the word. He came with a great reputation, particularly as a rugby player. He was a Liverpool man and had been "capped" for Lancashire. His appearance confirmed this by his flat nose and almost 'cauliflower' ears. Well over six feet tall, and with muscular weight to match, his physical appearance was formidable yet this was belied by an easy-going and friendly manner. Truly a delightful man to know'.*

He was killed in the most dreadful conditions by German Tiger Tanks firing their 88mm guns near the little village of Croce in Tuscany, Italy. He and a colleague were driving their tanks in a flanking manoeuvre around the back of the town when they were attacked. Major Zacharias died whilst helping his sergeant who was struck first. His loss was a dreadful blow to the whole squadron and both tanks were completely destroyed.

Died 7th September 1944 aged 30. Buried in the Coriano Ridge War Cemetery, Rimini (Ref. XVII.M6)

With thanks to John Zacharias, son of John Paul, Catherine Tattersall, daughter of Major Fearnley and the late Kay Slater.

John Paul Zacharias
1914–1944. *Courtesy of John Dale Zacharias.*

5 MORE ABOUT COATS OF ARMS

Until the Reformation, it was customary for churches to display a representation of Christ on the cross, with his Mother on one side and St John on the other. This was called the Rood, and was normally placed high above the screen which separated the nave (where the people sat) from the chancel/sanctuary (where the altar was situated). When Henry VIII took charge of the Church himself, roods were removed and replaced with his own coat of arms. The people had to face the King every morning! During the Commonwealth period, these earlier arms were mainly destroyed and replaced by the Commonwealth arms. At the Restoration of Charles II, Royal Arms were once again put up, but this time voluntarily.

At Sefton, there used to be a free-standing coat of arms on top of the rood screen, and it is featured in some paintings and early photographs. These arms, which were given to St Luke's Church in Formby, belonged to Victoria (1842). There is a painted board, about 56 inches wide by 60 inches high on the north wall – above the War Memorial. These appear to have been originally the Arms of William III. On the accession of Queen Anne in 1702, it is likely that a local painter was employed to 'bring them up to date' – so Anne's motto was probably painted over the bottom panel or it was replaced. Interestingly, Anne chose the same Latin motto as Elizabeth I – *Semper Eadem* (*Always the Same*). According to CEA Cheesman, Rouge Dragon Pursuivant in 2008, the arms are incorrect – the small shield in the middle of the main one should show the arms of the Duchy of Nassau (a blue background peppered with gold rectangles with a red lion on a gold background).

Royal Coat of Arms of Queen Anne

Despite these oddities, it is a charming record of how the royal progress of the country was marked in rural Sefton. The lion on the left is well animated with a terrifying roar and both the unicorn and lion display signs of male prowess which would cause blushes were they easier to view.

The painting is unvarnished and quite dull, with some loss of gold. In the 1990s it was conserved and stabilised.

5 GEORGE AUDLEY ESQ

George Audley, who is best remembered for donating the statues of Peter Pan and Eros in Sefton Park (in South Liverpool), was born in Park Street, Toxteth Park in 1864. He spent all his business life working for J. P. O'Brien and Co in Pall Mall, Liverpool, which was a general merchants but specialised in the export of beer and stout. Through his hard work, long hours and business sense, he rose to become managing director, and guided the company through some lucrative deals with Scotch whisky companies in Scotland. By 1920, he was able to retire a very wealthy man, and spent the rest of his life collecting mostly Victorian art and giving it away, as well as large chunks of money. He was a bachelor who had no interest in consolidating his fortune for future generations – the only future he saw was the provision of art for the people of Liverpool.

In 1924 he presented fourteen valuable paintings to the Walker Art Gallery, and a year later the Lord Mayor of Liverpool Sir Frederick Bowring gave £1000 with the promise to match any further donations. George Audley promptly gave £10,000, which was automatically doubled. Added to that he gave forty-three more pictures. Over the next fifteen years or so, he continued to give pictures in abundance, the best known being *Vespers*, by Singer Sargent (1928). A new gallery was named the Audley Gallery in his honour. He also gave statuary, such as John Gibson's *Garland Dance*, Arthur G. Walker's life-size *Adam and Eve*, and Spence's statue of *Flora Macdonald* (for the Sefton Park Palm House). He also gave a children's garden and floral clock to Stanley Park in North Liverpool and his famous collection of Toby Jugs to the Liverpool Museum. His best known and loved donations were the two copies of famous London sculptures for Sefton Park. He was criticised by living artists for commissioning expensive replicas, but he followed his own star.

Sefton Church was where his elder brother had been confirmed and, recognising its special qualities, he decided to make a gift of two religious paintings. At the time this was not a straightforward operation, and there is correspondence from the church expressing some grave reservations in accepting two paintings of the Virgin Mary which could be construed as *too Catholic*. In the end the paintings came and the Madonna Granducca had to hang in the Revestry where only the Rector could see it. Today, it is in the Lady Chapel, as already noted. Unfortunately, Botticelli's *Madonna* was destroyed by ingress of water and a modern print now takes its place in its magnificent frame.

'Te Deum' Window in loving memory of William and Anne Audley, given by their children. 1927.

Detail of the 'Te Deum' window showing the Doctors of the Church, left to right: St Augustine, Pope St Gregory, St Helen, St Jerome and St Ambrose.

69

When Audley died suddenly in Southport in 1932 he left a number of personal bequests to friends, a large donation to the building fund of the Anglican Cathedral, a choice of fifty paintings to the City of Liverpool, and the residue to Dr Barnardo's Homes. He loved Liverpool, children and art.

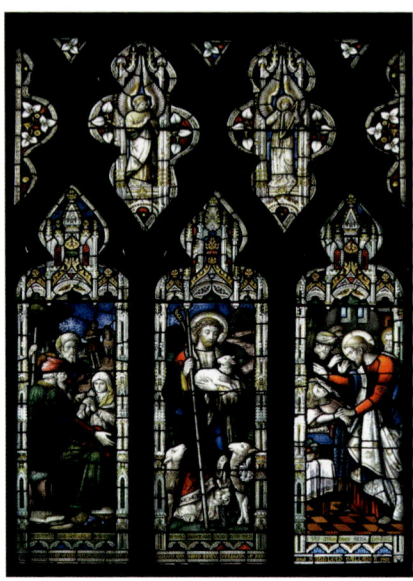

The Gallaher Window, with scenes from Isaiah, Mark and Kings. 1901.

TUDOR SCREENS 7

It is thought that the fine Tudor oak screen was erected before the Reformation and intended as a Rood Screen, to hold a Calvary on top. Most surviving rood screens have a staircase, but there is no trace of one at Sefton. Maybe it was made of wood and dismantled many years ago, or the Reformation intervened and it was never constructed. There are certainly no stone stairs, as is usually the case.

According to Caröe,[4] the renowned architect and author of the definitive work on Sefton Church (pages 15–17), the Sefton Pew once stood on the north side in front of the Blundell screen near where the pulpit stands today. He identified this position by examining the remaining parts of screens. He claims that in about 1820 it was moved – and damaged – when it was clumsily fitted in the south aisle under the heavy Georgian galleries. Until that time, the pulpit was in the nave attached to a column on the north side. The Sefton Pew was later moved again – into what was the Bulcley Chantry. As we will discover, the Mollinex Chantry was formerly also on the north side.

The fine woodwork was crudely painted and some of it grained after the Reformation, so that by the end of the eighteenth century, it was in a sorry state. In 1842–3, some new framework had to be inserted, and new and larger doors had to be made. Much of the carving is original, but new wood and lead had to be inserted in either 1820 or 1843.

The angels bearing shields depicting emblems of the Passion facing east and west are original. The pendants supporting shields show coats of arms. The original ones facing east belong to the Molyneux family, while those facing west are more modern and depict the Blundell and Rothwell families.

Detail of the gothic Tudor screen canopy.

Mr Dorning Rasbotham[5] in his *'Shorthand Collections'* of 1774 suggested that the screens were better, *'When its neighbouring lords preserved this decoration with pious care'*.

This rings true as the Molyneux family only sporadically visited the church during penal times, and from the mid-eighteenth century adopted St Chad's Church Kirkby, as their family church. The Blundells of Crosby ceased worshipping at Sefton after the Reformation (despite Nicholas the Diarist being Church Warden in 1714–15), and the Blundells of Ince only put in minimal attendance.

The writer of the *Illustrated Itinerary of the County of Lancashire 1842* found that,

'There is a fine carved canopy remaining over the pulpit, the workmanship of which is exceedingly beautiful, although much injured by time'.

Richard Bridgens in 1822 fortunately produced a folio of drawings. While some illustrations are not architecturally accurate, we can glimpse the arrangement of items as he found them.

The early sixteenth-century screen arcade (bottom) has been restored to its original glory by Caröe. In about 1820 it was inexplicably altered (top).

By the time that Caröe came into contact with the church (*c.*1893), much of the intrinsic beauty had been debased, although he recognised treasures underneath the wood-grain effect on some of the woodwork.

THE PULPIT

He that covereth his sinne shall not prosper,
But whoso confesseth and forsaketh them shall have
Mercie: happy is the man. Anno Domino, 1635.
(*Prov. 28,13*)

Round the canopy or sounding board, are the words:
My sonne, feare thou the Lorde and the Kinge
And medle not with them that are given to change.
(*Prov. 24,21*)

This last quotation is a warning in those dangerous times of civil strife.

The original position of
William Molyneux brass.

8 NICHOLAS BLUNDELL THE DIARIST

Church Affairs

Perhaps the most famous historical character connected with Sefton Church is Nicholas Blundell who was the Squire of Little Crosby in the early eighteenth century and despite being a Catholic, became Church Warden in 1714. Better still, he wrote a personal diary for 26 years, so we have a daily account of the church affairs for his year in office as well as a broader picture of Lancashire and national life. Duty done in April 1715, he was probably looking forward to developing his estates, but little did he know that a national crisis was looming which would engulf his lifestyle. The account of his subsequent trip to London before seeking refuge in the Low Countries is too interesting to miss – not many Sefton folk travelled so far at that time and only Nicholas' detailed account is extant.

The Jacobean pulpit.   Sounding board of the pulpit.

His Diary is a meticulous record of daily life in Lancashire, London and Flanders. From 27th July 1702 to 4th April 1728, he only missed one day and that was 20th January 1728. Its beauty, like most diaries, is that it was written for his own eyes only so it lacks guile and subterfuge. While he would most certainly recognise Sefton Church today and be pleased to see his own handiwork, he would, no doubt, be astonished if he were to venture into Liverpool – perhaps the only remaining vestige from his lifetime would be the Bluecoat Chambers, the original home of the school founded by the unrelated Bryan Blundell in 1708. That said, I am sure he would be excited and thrilled beyond belief.

Birth

His birth was announced in the *Great Hodge Podge*, another huge resource of materials started by his grandfather, who was known as 'The Cavalier':

> '*Nicholas Blundell born on the first day of September, 1669 being Wednesday just at 10 in the morning, the season being hot, dry and glorious*'.

Portrait of Nicholas Blundell the Diarist,
(1669–1737) Squire of Little Crosby.
Courtesy of Mark Blundell Esq.

He arrived into a family which was devoutly Catholic, and staunchly Recusant having suffered grievously during early penal times. His grandfather, and two earlier squires had languished in gaol, despite always being Royalists. Their lands had been sequestered and had to be bought back, and they had paid crushing fines for their refusal to attend the Church of England.

By the time Nicholas inherited from his grandfather in 1702, a more liberal mood was in the ascendancy, and apart from paying huge levies as a Papist and hiding from danger during the Jacobite uprising, he was able to enjoy much of his life.

His faith also gave him a distinct advantage: he was sent to school in St Omers in France to receive a Catholic education, which was far more liberal than that on offer in the English Public Schools. Female members of his family, including his two daughters, likewise benefitted as they enjoyed an education abroad at a time when girls were usually taught at home, or not at all. He also travelled abroad in later life with his daughters during the Jacobite Crisis and this made him a very enlightened and modern man.

With its legible writing, with eccentic and sometimes amusing and inconsistent spelling, his Diary[6] commences:

> *A Diurnall or a Daly Account wherein I have set down Something or Other every day . . .*

His method was to carry a small notebook, a *'fowl drought'* and later copy entries into his main diary. This he often found tiresome, but was able to pass many a rainy hour on the task.

He also kept detailed accounts of all his expenditure, and records of his tenants and land. He was always interested in modern methods and innovations, never missing an opportunity to learn new ways of improving his estate.

His detailed record of the weather with monthly summaries is most valuable and fascinating as weather was so important for people relying on the land for income.

Marriage

One urgent task was to find a wife with a good dowry and the strong possibility of an heir. Debts which mounted up during penal times had to be repaid, so he

Harbour view of Liverpool in the early eighteenth century.

needed £2,000 and a wife. Nicholas married Frances, daughter of Lord Langdale of Holme on 17th June 1703 – he was thirty-two and she was seventeen. She was his dear wife in terms of cost and patience. He and other family members, such as his mother and great aunt were sometimes driven to reside with other relatives in order to escape from her, and the village's much loved priest, Fr Aldred also left the Hall and moved into a cottage in the village. She was not easy to please.

Nevertheless, they produced two daughters, Mary and Frances, but sadly no son and heir. Despite his disappointment, he lavished his love and affection on these two girls, and when they were old enough, took them to school in Flanders for an education. He demanded that they should marry for love only, and was most upset when Mally (Mary) thought that she had a vocation to be a nun. Eventually they did marry for love – Mary to John Coppinger and Frances to Henry Peppard.

In Nicholas' last years, he was a doting grandfather to Stephen, son of Mary, and Christopher, son of Frances. Stephen died as a boy in 1745 and Christopher in 1771 without issue. The estate passed to Frances' third son, Nicholas in 1771, who took the name and arms of Blundell.

Most interesting to us here is the period 1714–1716 when Nicholas became Church Warden at Sefton and soon afterwards was forced to hide and flee from Crosby to avoid being associated with the Jacobite cause.

Church Warden

As the Squire of Little Crosby in the Parish of Sefton, he was expected to take a turn as Church Warden, which in those days was a civic as well as a religious duty.

Frances Blundell, daughter of
Marmaduke, 2nd Baron Langdale,
and wife of Nicholas Blundell.
Courtesy of Mark Blundell Esq.

Nicholas had a problem. Although he was on the best of social terms with all the local Anglican clergy, he was, after all, a Catholic. On returning from a visit to his manorial lands in Ditton on 30th March 1714, he arrived late at the parish meeting at Sefton Church, only to discover that he had been chosen Church Warden. This was a shock to him.

After the meeting he retired to the Church Inn (by the churchyard west wall) to have a drink with the two parsons and others from the meeting. After some soul-searching, on 1st April, he was off to Ormskirk to consult with a Mr Brooks about the situation. Resolved not to accept the position, the following day he visited Sefton to inform Parson Letus of his decision, but finding him not at home, managed to find the Clerk, William Harrison, and informed him, in the presence of a witness. On 3rd April he went to see John Sumner of Moorhouses to ask him to stand in temporarily, but found him also not at home. Getting somewhat desperate, on 5th April he set out for Chester to consult Richard Boucher (a lawyer and proctor of the Abbey Court). Boucher's fee is recorded later as 3s 6d. Before he left, he bought some gloves for his wife and left his leather breeches to be cleaned (cost 4s 6d).

On the night of 13th April he was prescribed pills by Dr Cawood, most likely to calm him down. By 16th April he thought he was in luck, as John Sumners agreed to act '*in part*' as Church Warden for him, which probably entailed the religious duties. The following day he was quite happily drinking in Liverpool with three parsons.

On 19th April he was taking more prescribed pills, but we never learn whether they were successful. By 21st April, he had come to terms with his destiny, and was ready to meet his co-Warden, Thomas Syer, at the Church Inn. They went into the church:

21 April 1714 '. . . we caused a Chest over the Church Pourch to be brock open as had not ben open'd of very many years . . .'.

It was not all doom and gloom for Nicholas: being Church Warden gave him a new legal power in this Anglican church. His grandfather, 'The Cavalier', had been involved in a legal dispute about his share of repairs to the church and churchyard in 1684/5 and had claimed that the money was being diverted to make a new road to the mill. By breaking open the chest and retrieving the Church Wardens' Accounts, Nicholas could now find out where the money had been spent. On 8th

May, Mr Lunt visited Nicholas and was asked to make copies of the Wardens' Accounts. In fact, he had two years copied (Easter 1684 to Easter 1686) and these are now the earliest Church Wardens' accounts extant. (Lancashire Archives (DDBL/31/4).

The Angel Inn in Dale Street Liverpool once frequented by Nicholas Blundell.

Accepting his new position, he flung himself wholeheartedly into it. During his year of office, he accomplished much and even managed to have a summer holiday in Yorkshire. He was the proactive lead Warden with Thomas Syer following on behind. His greatest achievements seem to have been setting up a Select Vestry of Twelve Gentlemen to represent the Parish, refurbishing the windows, roofs and pulpit, erecting a Benefactors' Table and designing and supervising the making of a Parish Hearse.

As a Catholic, he avoided services in the Church, apart from burials. Instead, there are frequent references to attending 'prayers', 'Masses' and 'Vespars' at his own house, the Grange at Alt, Lydiate Hall, the New House, or Fr Aldred's Chapel in Little Crosby. Most gentry visitors to Crosby Hall ended up in the latter place. When on 14th October he received the late 'Doctor Lathoms Box of Church-stuff', he lent some of it to Fr Aldred.

Surprisingly, he is frequently entertaining, or being entertained by Anglican Clergy, on one occasion dining with no fewer than five clergymen. While he was religious, he was no fanatic, so it is amusing to find him taking delivery (30th October) of a new saddle, '*as the Catholick Sadler of Chorley has made for me*'.

Between Church business, Nicholas continued in his busy schedule of meetings, agricultural affairs, social excursions and funerals. It is remarkable how much travelling he managed, considering the state of the roads and bridle paths. When alone, he went on horseback, but a carriage was often used for family events. Sometimes family members would walk several miles to an engagement, and the coach would be dispatched to bring them home. He often called such a social visit a *How-do-you*. Interestingly on 3rd May he went to visit his relatives at Scarisbrick Hall, but soon after dinner Mr Scarisbrick had to attend a business meeting regarding Martin Mere (which was drained later in the century). Funerals often provided a useful forum for members of all the leading families.

Nicholas Blundell's hatchment, showing his coat of arms.

By the end of the first month of Office, 30th April, he met Thomas Syer in Liverpool and bought two locks for the church, and promised the plumbing and glazing work to Richard Eccleston, who 'treated' them. This so-called *treat* would have implications later. While in town, they popped into the Old Church (St Nicholas') at the Pierhead to look at the Legacy Table, which gave him an idea.

Displaying a painted board in the Church denoting legacies and gifts would encourage parishioners to give generously. This idea he pursued, designing and executing it. On 11th February 1715 he spent most of the afternoon drawing it out and on 20th showed it to Thomas Syer. On 12th April, he gave orders for it to be hung on the church wall (see illustration on page 64).

On 1st May 1714, the Wardens were in the Church Inn (often called 'Harsnops' after the landlord John Harsnop or Harsnip) to collect the Church Leys, but with few customers. With free time on their hands, they were able to examine all the church windows. Nicholas also signed a petition for Thomas Bradley to get a pew (he was successful). The Church Leys were paid via the Constable during the following months in dribs and drabs.

The Blue Coat Hospital, Liverpool (by Herdman).
Nicholas Blundell would still recognise it today.

On 12th May, he was resident in Harsnops to finalise the accounts of the previous Wardens and while there, asked Richard Webster to make some iron work for the font, giving him detailed instructions.

Holding manorial rights in Ditton, Nicholas also owned a pew in Farnworth Church (Widnes). On 13th May he applied (successfully) to the Bishop's Court, sitting in Ormskirk, for permission to put doors without locks on his pew. He and a party from Sefton later dined at the 'Talbot' in Ormskirk and that night Mrs Ann Molyneux and her sister Bridget stayed the night at the Hall. In 1732, the same Ann Molyneux was to leave a large bequest of £40 to buy a silver chalice and make the altarpiece (reredos). This donation is inscribed on the Benefactors' board.

By Autumn, Nicholas had obviously decided what needed to be done at Sefton Church, so on 5th October, he visited Thomas Syer at Great Crosby, before going on to a workshop to see how his plans for a 'Corps Carriage' and the new 'Pulpit Stayers' were coming on. Nicholas was in the habit of generously lending his own hearse for funerals at Sefton, but thought the church should have its own.

These jobs were supervised closely by Nicholas, who must have annoyed the craftsmen by his frequent visits and attention to detail.

A Visit to Yorkshire

The summer months were good for travelling, as the roads were better compacted and the days longer and warmer. After having a 'Swarme of Bees' for two days on 15th and 16th June, the following day saw Nicholas, his wife and daughter Mary set off for a visit to Stockhild, the family home of his wife, and then York. At Stockhild, Mary drank the sulphur spa water. At York, the couple went with Lady Smithson to visit Mrs Fairfax and later Mr Charles Fairfax dined with them at Stockhild. After visits to Harrogate and Dewsbury, they arrived back at Crosby at midnight on 6th July, but this did not stop Nicholas setting to work scything his cole-seed before he went to bed. His brother Joseph had returned with them.

The shrine at Holywell in Flintshire was a favourite place for Catholics, and its waters were thought to have powers to cure. The Blundells still wanted a male heir so Mrs Blundell often made pilgrimages to bathe. On 24th July, Mrs Blundell, Mally (Mary) and brother Joseph, now a Jesuit priest left Nicholas in Liverpool and set out for Holywell – a journey which involved crossing two rivers. Nicholas remained in Liverpool that evening and saw '*the Show of Waterworks at the Griffan*'. Arriving home late, he found an unexpected guest come to lodge (Sir James Poole). The other family members returned safely on the 26th July.

The next day, after enjoying a full day out and a '*Silly-bub*' at Charles Howerd's, Nicholas got news of his '*Brother Midleton's Funerall*' in Stockhild and so he set out at eleven o'clock at night on horseback, arriving at Bolton at 6.00 am. After a well-deserved rest, off he went to Bradford where he lodged at the Black Swan. He met the family the next day and obviously paid his respects, but does not mention the funeral. On 30th July he started his journey home, staying that

The Minster at York.

night in Skipton, before arriving in Preston where he bought some Delphinium flower roots and visited old Mrs Walmesley of Showley. The next day, he attended a funeral Mass in Preston for a Mr Knight and met old Mr Walmesley before travelling home via Ormskirk.

In the days before cameras and photocopiers, documents had to be copied by hand, so on 3rd August, Nicholas spent most of the afternoon copying the previous year's Church Wardens' Accounts. On 21st August he was in Lancaster, attending some trials. In particular he notes the case of Williamson vs Rushton and records that Williamson was awarded £160 (an enormous sum). On the way home he lodged in Preston at Mr Jackson's and '*saw some tricks of Legerdemesney and a Woman dance with Swords & Tankerds*'. Back home, he took his wife and daughters to Ormskirk Fair on 30th August and showed his children the '*Strange Creatures . . . a Tyger, a Sivet Cat*', and the tricksters from Preston: the woman doing her dancing and her husband '*playing Tricks of Leger-de-mesney*'.

The Scottish Play

There was also entertainment near home. Receiving a ticket for a play in Liverpool from Mrs Ann Molyneux, on 13th October, Nicholas, his wife and Mally dined at Much Woolton, before heading to the New-Market Theatre to see '*a Play Acted called Mackbeth*', (the earliest known Shakespeare performance in Liverpool).

It was back to church business on 21st October when Nicholas went to Harsnops to discuss a broken bell wheel in the church tower. On 25th, both Wardens were summoned to Parson Letus' house to examine Richard Eccleston and the Clerk about their bill for plumbing. Perhaps the Wardens' *treat* on 30th April had been added to the final bill.

On 3rd November, he visited Sefton to see Richard Heaton and John Melling working on the new bell wheel while on the following day he received an invitation to solemnise a priest's jubilee. Then on 5th November he was back at Harsnops to view the new bell wheel, and saw a Mr Ralf Marser who '*took a peal at Ringing*'. On 9th he dined at Newhouse for the Jubilee with Mr Scarisbrick, Sir Francis Anderton and several priests.

During December, he was busy supervising church work such as the hearse and pulpit stairs, and even bought the wine from the *Talbot*, in Liverpool for the Christmas obligation. Sadly, on

Church Warden's Pew
(drawn by E. J. A. Caröe)

23rd December, Mrs Molyneux from Alt Grange died. On Christmas Eve he went to her home to pray and heard three Masses, as well as helping to say the *Officium Defunctorum*. Although strange to us, the funeral took place on Christmas Day, and Nicholas attended the Requiem Mass at Alt Grange, but did not go to the grave at Sefton as he had a visitor at home. The actual burial would likely have been simply a practical affair – all the religious rites having been done beforehand.

In the Holydays after Christmas, the two Molyneux boys from Croxteth came to stay – their father Lord Molyneux having to stay at home with the gout.

On 1st January (New Year's Day was then 25th March), Nicholas looked at the church accounts and devised new laws '*to be made for the good of the Parish*'. By 5th January, agreement was reached on a form of Select Vestry. Although it is not mentioned after his term of Office, it seems likely that a Vestry was formed and Nicholas was a member of it.

Nicholas was fond of card games and tricks so he was pleased on 13th January when Fr Aldred '*set a Hen-Egg upon an end on a Looking Glass, (and) he shew'd me the way*'. After practising, on 21st January he proudly notes, '*I set an Egg upon one End tis the first time I did it*'. He was also keen on mixing medicines, and sometimes acted like the local physician. On 26th January he records: '*I gave a Poore Woman a Doce for the Falling Sickness*'. On 1st February there was a massive storm in Lancashire which wreaked havoc. The following day, William Atherton came from Ditton to give a report on the damage there, but hearing of sickness, Nicholas dispensed *'some Phisick ... for three that had the Ague-Fits'*.

During early Spring, there was much work to complete, and Nicholas went to see Parson Richmond about the parish affairs and then to Chester to consult with Mr Boucher. It seems that he had sought help in drawing up a petition to the Bishop of Chester about the Select Vestry for on 9th April he showed it to Parson Letus and his co-warden Thomas Syer. On 11th April, Parson Richmond formally proposed the idea at the Parish Meeting.

As Easter approached, time was running out: he had to check progress on the hearse, the pulpit and see the Table of Benefactors hung. On 13th April he was working on the Parish Accounts and two days later adjusting them: for once rain was welcome, *'It Rained pritty much almost all day which was very acceptable'*.

The final day came, and on 19th he delivered the accounts and *'severall Stints were set for the better Regulation the Affairs of the Parish'*. He also *'gave Parson Letus £5 towards the Augmentation of the Parish Stock'*, whereby getting his own name listed on the Benefactors' Table.

It must have been a relief to sign off the Accounts and hand on the rôle to his successor. During the rest of the month, it was business as usual: on 20th he sowed some asparagus seeds, on 22nd he was pleased that he, *'observed the great Eclips of the Sun'*, and on 24th his daughter Frances went to the seashore – not to bathe or enjoy the air, but to see the body of a man who had been washed up. Life goes on, but soon national events were to change this domestic bliss at least for a couple of years. The Stuart Rebellion was heading south.

The Sefton Shore, largely unchanged apart from the distant appearance of Blackpool.

A Streat Place for a fat Man

Jacobites were made up mainly of three groups: English Catholics, High Anglicans and members of the Church of Scotland. Nicholas was therefore in the firing line, particularly as his wife was related to the wife of the Earl of Derwentwater, a leading Jacobite.

In August, he had an unwelcome visitor:

18th August: 'Henry Valentine the High Constable serched here for Horses, Arms and Gunpowder'.

On 5th September 1715, Nicholas was giving directions to a lawyer to settle his estate, which was ready for inspection on 27th September.

On 21st October: '*I perused a Deed of Settlement . . . for me provided I dye without issou-male . . . I got in the last of my Oats*'. The juxtaposition here would have passed over Nicholas' head.

By 29th October, danger was drawing nearer:
'*We expected the Hors Militia to come and serch here*'.

In November, he announces the conflict:
12th November: '*The Fight at Preston was begun*', and the following day, he was swamped:

13th November: '*This Hous was twice sirched by some Foot as came from Leverpoole, I think the first party were about twenty six*'.

While there is no evidence anywhere in the extensive family records of sympathy for the Jacobite Rebellion, Nicholas realised that his religion alone could possibly convict him. In reality, he was only interested in practising his faith in private, and caring for his family, his tenants and land. During earlier, harsher times, his house was equipped with '*priest-holes*' – places where a man could hide in safety for several days. On 16th November, he records perhaps the most famous entry in his diaries, and one which combines gravity with humour:

Pew ends (Bridgens).

16th November: '*I set in a Streat place for a fat Man*'.

Here he stayed for several days on and off – reading books such as *England's Jests* and *The English Rogue*. On 19th November, the house was searched again, and on the following day, he was in the '*Boys Chamber*' and '*heard him talk*' – probably the searcher was very close. On the same day, another person was hiding in a nearby hole:

20th November: '*I had a Bed-Fellow*', which might have been Fr Aldred, their priest, or more likely a fugitive from the fighting in Preston. On 21st November, he and his bed-fellow parted, and he probably came out of hiding.

He had obviously decided to flee to the continent with his family, but first he had to travel to London and wait for a *pass* to leave the country. London, being the metropolis, was relatively safe: it was crowded with people, and well away from Catholic Lancashire. His *Pass* was obtained with the help of a lawyer from Liverpool.

Leaving '*Runkhorn*' on 24th November, his journey was long and complicated, but he finally arrived in London on 2nd December, lodging at Captain Stevens' house near Gray's Inn Passage.

81

London

On 9th December, he witnessed the rebel leaders arrive:

9th December: 'I saw the Preston Prisoners come into Town'. On 23rd, he also: *'. . . saw five Men and Two Women carted towards Tibourne there to be executed'*.

Nicholas enjoyed being in the Capital with all its attractions. His priest, Fr Aldred was also there and on 22nd December they were to enjoy an outing with the attraction of *'pail Ailes'*. He also went to see the new St Paul's Cathedral and the *'moving Picturs in Smithfield'*.

Nicholas was keen to see the new
St Paul's Cathedral in London.

It was a bitter winter and the Thames was frozen solid. On 4th January he went to Southwark and *'saw severall walking upon the ice above the Bridge'*. This must have reminded him of home and Sefton Meadows. On 19th January, he himself ventured upon the ice and tasted an ox roast, freshly cut.

He started to learn French, fixed his landlady's clock, changed the locks on his doors after having them picked, and treated a local family to *'a Shew of Monstures'*. At the end of December he had seen the *'Moving Picturs in Smithfield'* and on 13th January he *'saw the Moving Images in Stanlow Street . . . the first time they were Shewed'*. He marvelled at a looking glass on sale at the Royal Exchange which in one piece measured 86 inches long and 44 inches wide and cost a staggering £130.

The end of January (30th), was the first time since the frost that boats could pass safely above London Bridge.

February 5th brought news that the Pretender and the Rebels had fled from Perth, but on 24th February, the Lords Derwentwater and Kenmure were executed. On 27th, he attended, *'a High-Mass for Lord Derwinwater at the French Envoys'*, and observes that *'Severall Persons of Note were there'*. (Embassies were legally entitled to maintain their own Chapels and priests).

Never one to miss an opportunity, he made enquiries about the Hamburg Lottery, before receiving his passport on 5th March. He had to pack now, but the following day he was able to see Mr Thomas Walmesley of Showley in Lancashire, finishing the day seeing *'the Apparitions in the Air lick Clowds of Fier & smoke'*.

Despite boarding the boat – the *St John of Bruges* – on the 12th March, bad weather delayed his departure, and he finally arrived on 15th March – after three nights on board but only 36 hours under sail.

Flanders

Flanders in those days was a little England over the sea, a microcosm of English Catholic Society. For Nicholas, it was a second home – a reminder of his youth and school days, and also the home of many older members of his family in convents. There were many English Catholic institutions, such as schools and convents like the *Convent des Dames Anglaises* in Bruges. He enjoyed sightseeing and daily life with his usual vigour – visiting the magnificent cathedrals, abbeys and churches and making devotions. During a period of four days in July, he visited 30 churches. He must have often thought about Sefton Church during this time.

Our Lady's Church Antwerp (now the Cathedral). Nicholas Blundell climbed over 600 steps to the top of the tower in August 1715.

Little Crosby village church.

One major problem for his diary was that Catholic Flanders was operating on the Gregorian Calendar (*new style*) while England was still resisting it and using the Julian Calendar. Flanders was in time ahead of England, so days had been *lost*. Nicholas recorded both dates just to be sure. England eventually had to capitulate and reluctantly adopted the new calendar of Pope Gregory in September 1752.

On 6th July, his wife and children arrived at Dunkirk on the *Harris Ship*, accompanied by John Gillibrand from Crosby. The two girls were destined to stay in Flanders until 1723 for a convent education (which was technically illegal). On 31st July 1717 he settled his children in their convent at Gravelines. The following day on 1st August 1717, Nicholas and Frances boarded the *Betty Yot,* which despite springing a leak and being delayed, sailed on 3rd August, and arrived in Margate on 5th August. Arriving by boat in London, nobody seemed to notice his missing girls, although the Customs' Officers no doubt were well rewarded by Nicholas.

Antwerp Cathedral's tower is the height of Salisbury's spire.

Home

He was later to return to Flanders in 1723 to collect his daughters, which would be his last visit abroad.

He died at Crosby in 1737 and was buried with his family in the Blundell Chapel at Sefton Church.

8 AN EARLY OPERATION: STONE IN BLUNDELL CHAPEL

It is remarkable to have details of an early operation on a tombstone. Obviously a devoted Molyneux servant, she was treated as if she were a member of the family and sent to Wigan. Sadly she did not survive for long, but the fact that she lasted almost two months is a great achievement.

Here lieth ye body of Mrs Teresa Booth who went to Wigan upon ye 28th of Octobr being St Simon and Judes day to have her breast cut for a cancer which was taken off ye 9th of Novbr and she died the 30th of Decbr 1717 in ye 42nd year of her age.

"Requiescat in Pace"

She was house keeper at Croxteth.

9 MORE ABOUT THE KNIGHTS

'Crusader' knight in canopied recess.

It is possible that these two effigies were originally sited in the Chancel, as that area was built and owned by the Molyneux Family. Churches are spaces for the living as well as the dead, and over the centuries, priorities change. It might have become inconvenient to have two large effigies blocking the route to the altar, and so they had to be moved.

At Sefton, the effigies obviously did not start out life in their present situation, for instance the canopy was not made for the figure which lies beneath it. You will notice that the figure is too long, and the niche has been crudely adapted. The canopied niche itself is also a mystery, although other examples are known throughout the country. They are always built into the north wall, whether outside or inside. The most likely explanation is that it is an '*Easter Sepulchre*', similar to the ones at Staunton St John's Oxfordshire and Herstmonceaux, Sussex.

The two knights: brothers in death.

Thomas Fiennes, 8th Baron Dacre in his will of September 1st 1531, made provision for his own tomb in Sussex, and also for a '*Sepulchre of Our Lord*'.

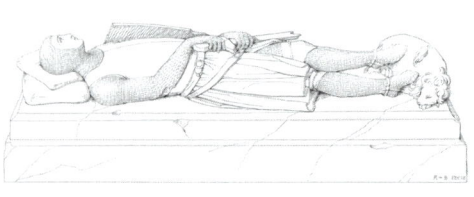

Molyneux Knight (Bridgens).

These were areas created for an Easter tableau of the resurrection (an empty tomb) or sometimes where a pyx and crucifix were deposited in solemn manner on Good Friday. The priest would pronounce: 'Surrexit, non est hic' (*He is risen, he is not here*). This is the all-important moment in the Christian journey so it is not surprising that some churches might have wished to create a permanent memorial.

While the canopied knight bears a Cross Moline, the second effigy is even less certain, as there are no distinguishing family symbols. His plate armour and beard, however, would seem to place him 1325–40 as beards were temporarily in fashion during that short period. He could possibly be the last Molyneux Lord of Little Crosby, Sir John Molyneux whose daughter Agnes married a Blundell and inherited the manor. The most interesting feature of this effigy is that he is resting his feet on a bent human figure (now largely missing), which needs little explanation.

10 NATHANIEL HITCH 1845–1937 SCULPTOR

Nathaniel Hitch was not a name known at Sefton but thanks to the research work of Gordon Lawson of Leeds, work in the church and on the war memorial can be linked to his name. He was born at Ware in Hertfordshire in 1845 and was the son of a joiner and carpenter. He must have inherited his father's handicraft skills because as a twelve-year-old he built a model of Ware church which is still displayed there. He was apprenticed probably at the age of thirteen or fourteen to

Carved altarpiece in the Lady Chapel.

a firm of wood carvers in London – Farmer & Brindley of Westminster Bridge Road. He was clearly well taught in a firm which produced work for the foremost architects of the day. After completing his apprenticeship he became a journeyman (literally being paid by the day) working for another London carver, Thomas Nicholls, who was working for the architect William Burgess on the lavishly carved interior of Cardiff Castle.

Eventually, he set up his own workshop at 60, Harleyford Road, Battersea and worked for many notable architects of the late nineteenth and early twentieth centuries. Among them was John Pearson (1817–1897) who was one of the most distinguished architects of the English 'Gothic Revival'. Pearson produced the first report on the conservation of Sefton Church in 1892 and his scheme was followed broadly by William Caröe in his work here from 1907 onwards. Caröe as a young architect was under his tutelage. Thanks to Pearson's high opinion of

Hitch's craftsmanship and artistry it was not surprising that Caröe was happy to commission work from him. Caröe's first job for him was at 78–83 Duke Street, London, and thereafter Hitch worked on a wide range of church commissions including work in the North West at Huyton Reformed Church, the Lady Chapel of St Margaret, Bodelwyddan and All Saint's Gresford near Wrexham.

At Sefton, the Lady Chapel altarpiece was given by the Countess of Sefton in memory of her daughter in 1918. The reredos is one of the great beauties of the church and once was ascribed to an unknown Italian sculptor. Possibly this was because it has some stylistic similarities to the elaborate frame which surrounds the copy of the Raphael painting in the south aisle. In fact, Nathanial Hitch carved the reredos and this is made clear in a letter from Caröe to the then rector, Canon Wells on 20th January 1921. It reads: '*Hitch did the sculpture in the Lady Sefton's reredos . . .*' This letter was in connection with his sculpture that tops the war memorial. Caröe was explaining how he commissioned Hitch directly rather than going through the main contractors for the erection of the memorial. Hitch lived to the grand age of 92 and was still working the year before his death.

MADONNA DEL GRANDUCA, AFTER RAPHAEL

The original painting hangs in the Pitti Gallery (Pitti Palace) in Florence and is priceless. It was probably painted in 1505, shortly after Raphael arrived in Florence. He was probably influenced in his use of *sfumato* by seeing the great paintings of Leonardo Da Vinci there. *Sfumato* is the technique of toning down, or *to evaporate like smoke*. There are no harsh outlines, a good example being the *Mona Lisa*. The original painting belonged to Ferdinand III Grand Duke of Tuscany, from whom it got its name.

THE MOLLINEX (OR MULLINEX) CHANTRY

The idea of singing Masses for the souls of the dead and even the living goes back to the early church. A priest was employed to sing Mass daily and sometimes he was expected to teach grammar to the local children. Money, land and buildings were given to provide an income for the priest and some chantries became rich and powerful. This attracted the eye of Henry VIII who set about destroying them. At Sefton there were at least two Chantries, both founded on the eve of the Reformation, so they were short-lived.

The Mollinex Chantry was situated in what is now the Lady Chapel and was founded by Margaret Bulcley's nephew, Rector Edward Molyneux about 1535. Its only priest, Thomas Kirkby, was charged '*to celebrate there for his* (Edward's) *soule*'. It would have been equipped with all things necessary for the celebration of the Mass yet when the commissioners arrived about 1548, their search for plate (silverware) produced 'none'.[7]

Under Edward VI, it was abolished and its income was assessed at £5 18s 7d. As compensation, Kirkby received 'a certain annuity or yearly pension to the determination of his life' to the value of £5.

The Reformation swept both chantries at Sefton away,[8] and much damage was done at Sefton with the destruction of artefacts. John Weever (1576–1632) accuses the reformers of 'leaving religion naked, bare and unclad; as Dionysius left Jupiter without a cloak and Esculapius without a beard'.

John Weever was born in Preston. His work, *Ancient Funerall Monuments* includes a portrait of him with this doggerel verse:

Choir Stalls.

> *Lancashire gave him breath,*
> *And Cambridge education.*
> *His studies are of Death.*
> *Of Heaven his meditation.*

0, 4 THE MOLYNEUX CHALICES

A notorious informer called Richard Hitchmough of Garston who was an ex-secular priest, provides us with a glimpse of Church Plate, one piece of which may have been used in the Mollinex Chantry at Sefton Church, in Sefton Hall Chapel, and most certainly at Croxteth.

'One large silver chalice, double gilt within with gold; one large paten of pure gold'.

There were also: 'Two silver crucibles, alias cruets, for wine and water: one silver plate, upon which the said crucibles used to stand; six tall silver candlesticks; and a large silver crucifix; the whole solid silver'. Hitchmough claimed that the first wife of Lord Molyneux stated that the plate had cost his Lordship £500 in London and that he had often seen it when he was Chaplain to his lordship in 1709.

What happened next is open to speculation, but it is likely that the chalice was removed from Croxteth in 1769, the year that Charles William, the 9th Viscount conformed to the Established Church.

In 1875, Rev Edward Powell, later parish priest at Lydiate, saved an old silver chalice from being scrapped by a dealer. Standing 7½ inches high and weighing 13 ounces, it is of silver but bears no

The Molyneux Chalice.
Courtesy of Liverpool Metropolitan Cathedral.

87

St Benet's Chalice and Patten.
*Courtesy of Liverpool
Metropolitan Cathedral.*

hallmarks and is probably English. Antiquarian experts have dated it to the early sixteenth century or a little earlier. The bowl and underside of the foot show hammer marks very distinctly. On each of the seven faces of the knop of the stem is engraved a quatrefoil ornament, and on the upper side of the foot a Calvary Cross. On the underside of the foot is engraved in Roman capital lettering of the period:

EX DONO D.C. MOLINEUX DNO
RICHARD HOLME
ANGLO=BENEDEDO 1697

The giver of the chalice was Caryll, 3rd Viscount Molyneux (buried at Sefton), whose son was said to have bought the plate described above. The recipient was Rev Richard Holme (or Helme) a Benedictine priest born in Goosnargh, and Chaplain at Sefton Hall Croxteth 1697–1715, before moving to Woolton Hall (on account of the Jacobite Uprising) where he died in 1717. There is also a paten of *c.*1620 and a silver ciborium which though unmarked is thought to have been made by Benjamin Pyne. The ciborium, which came from the parish of St Swithin Gillmoss, has an inscription which reads: †*The Gift of ye Hon Mary Molyneux to Croxteth 1738. Pray for her.*

The Molyneux Ciborium.
*Courtesy of Liverpool
Metropolitan Cathedral.*

Another intriguing silver gilt chalice from the early 16th century belongs to the parish of St Benet in nearby Netherton. On its foot is inscribed *A†S 1693*, which refers to the Rev Andrew Shirley who was Chaplain to Lord Molyneux at Sefton Hall. There is also a paten inscribed *A†S.*

There is a strong possibility that these chalices were used in Sefton Church until the Commissioners arrived, before being removed to Sefton Hall, Croxteth Hall and St Benet's Chapel in Netherton.

Today, they are all on public display in the Treasury of the Metropolitan Cathedral in Liverpool (see illustrations).

The Molyneux Ton

PISCINAE

When in use, they have a drain which goes straight down into the earth, so that after the priest washes his fingers with holy water, the surplus is washed directly into the earth. They were originally sited near the altar so that the priest could use them immediately after the service. There is a common misconception that consecrated elements were poured away into the piscina, but this is against Canon Law and untrue.

The one here at Sefton appears to have been used in conjunction with the original altar in this chapel. The floor has been raised considerably (see level of Knight's recess). After the Reformation, they generally fell into disuse, but this highly decorative one remains in this atmospheric part of the church.

12 THE EAST WINDOW

This was given in 1870 in memory of Rev R. R. Rothwell, Rector. The remains of the previous window are in the Molyneux Chapel and in the south windows.

The upper tracery has IHS in the centre at the very top in a dove shaped light. Below this, there is a dove surrounded by four angels.

At the top on either side are two stags' heads each with a shield beneath. The Stag's head is the Rothwell family crest and below is their coat of arms. There are four angels in the lights above the side panels.

The four foil arches have more angels. The rest of the upper tracery bears acanthus leaves: a symbol of Christian belief in the resurrection.

The Panels – Each of the panels bears an inscription.

Above the main mullion – Christ is in the centre with two scenes from

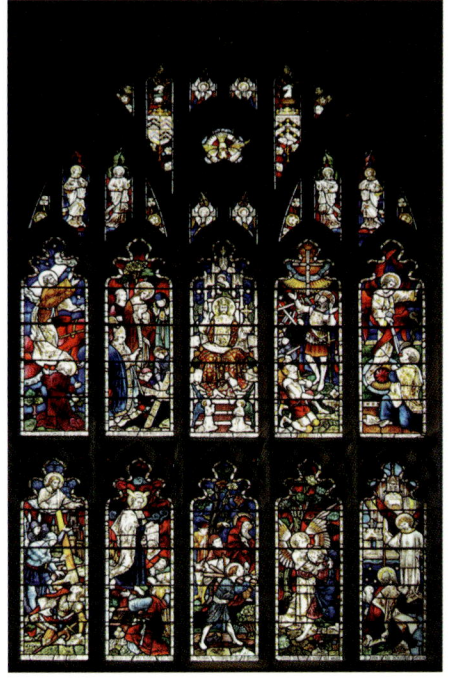

The East Window.

history on either side and flanked by two Old Testament prophets (from left to right):

1 *The Translation of Elijah* Elijah going to heaven in a chariot. Elijah did not die but was taken up to heaven whilst still alive. (2 Kings 2 v 1–11)

2 *St Helen finding the True Cross* St Helen is believed to have found the cross on which Jesus was crucified around AD 327 in Jerusalem.

3   *Our Saviour in Majesty* The risen and ascended Christ is seen seated on a throne, holding an orb in one hand with the other raised in blessing. There are two angels at his feet.

4   *Vision of the Cross to Constantine* Constantine, St Helen's son saw a vision of the Cross of Christ before he went into battle against Maxentius. He won the battle and become the sole emperor of the Roman Empire.

5   *Isaiah is touched with a live coal* Isaiah is seen kneeling before an angel who is touching his tongue with a flame. The angel cauterises Isaiah's lips to enable him to speak on behalf of God. (Isaiah 6 v 6–10)

Below the main mullion – three Old Testament patriarchs at significant incidents are flanked by two New Testament apostles and writers.

From left to right:

1   *Conversion of St Paul* Paul is blinded by a light from heaven. Saul was converted to belief in Christ by this vision and his name changed from Saul to Paul. He is seen kneeling with two Roman Soldiers. (Acts of the Apostles 9 v 1–19)

2   *Moses with the tablets of the Law* He holds up a stone bearing Roman numerals 1–10 to represent the ten Commandments. He is surrounded by kneeling men. (Exodus 20 v 1–20)

3   *Abraham on his way to Mount Moriah* Abraham was commanded by God to sacrifice his son (hence the position of this below Christ). Abraham is riding a donkey and his son Isaac is carrying the sticks for the fire. At the last moment Abraham is stopped and a lamb is substituted for sacrifice.

4   *Jacob wrestling with the Angel* Jacob sustained a dislocated hip in the fight and God changed his name to Israel, becoming the Father of the Nation. (Gen 32 v 22–31)

5   *St John on Island of Patmos* St John the Divine was exiled to Patmos off the coast of Turkey. Here he had visions and wrote the book of Revelation. He is kneeling in front of an Angel and holding a scroll. His symbol, an Eagle, is on the left , at the top the *lamb who was slain* (Rev 6), and below scenes from Revelation of the New Jerusalem (Rev 21 v 1–6) (Courtesy of Helen Hunter).

Chancel and Sanctuary

Edward Morton D.D.

His monument has a long Latin inscription which is translated as:

Sacred to the pious memory of Edward Morton, S.T.P., son of, and at length heir, of William Morton Esq., of Moreton, in the County of Chester, formerly a fellow of King's College, Cambridge, and also a Prebendary of the Cathedral of Chester, who, for the thirty-six years more or less not even those being left out in which he lived as if a banished man, despoiled of all his goods, was wont anxiously to rule this church of fortune, by no means equally a sharer but to either equal. He who well knew how to use prosperity soberly, and, more, adversity bravely. A constant maintainer of primitive piety, and, moreover, learning, he was all but a martyr. Assuredly a bright and rare example. He died February 28th, in the year of our Lord 1674, and in the year of his age 76.

His most sorrowful wife Margaret daughter of Sir William Webb caused this monument to be placed to her most beloved husband.

2 MEMORIALS

There are various interesting memorials on the walls of the Sanctuary and Chancel.

Rothwell Monument and Hatchments

An impressive marble memorial may be seen on the north wall of the chancel erected by Rector Richard Rothwell and dedicated in 1844 to fourteen members of his family. Many of them, including the Rector himself, are buried beneath the monument.

Two impressive hatchments belonging to the Rothwells can be seen high up on either side of the chancel. They display the motto:

Virtuti Fortuna Comes (*sic*) *Fortune is companion to valour*

The north Chancel wall with the Rothwell Monument.

Rev Richard Rainshaw Rothwell, Rector of Sefton:

Sacred to the memory of the Hon. Richard Rainshaw Rothwell MA for 50 years Rector of this parish born January 27th 1771, died April 25th 1863.

Richard Rainshaw Rothwell, Marquis De Rothwell and Martha Lydiard, Marchioness de Rothwell

Sacred to the memory of Martha Lydiard, Marchioness de Rothwell Born 5th January 1821 fell asleep 28th June 1885

"Blessed are the dead which die in the Lord" Rev. XIV 13

And of Richard Rainshaw Rothwell Marquis de Rothwell who died March 11th 1890 aged 81 years

The Rothwell Patrons and Rectors and their connections (Rectors are in bold). Ω = buried at Sefton.

James Rothwell (bought Advowson of Sefton in 1747) married Sarah Rainshaw of Manchester in 1718.

Their son was **Rev Richard Rothwell 1723–1801 (Rector 1763–1801).**

His son was **Rev Richard Rainshaw Rothwell 1771–1863 (Rector 1801–1863)** Ω – see his hatchment in the chancel.

Rev Roger Dawson-Duffield, Count of Monaco **(Rector 1863–1871)** was a friend of Richard Rainshaw Rothwell (1st Marquis) Ω.

A Rothwell Hatchment.

The Rothwell Monument.

Rev Englebert Horley (Rector 1871–1883) = Martha Rothwell (born 1850), daughter of Ralph Rothwell Ω (1816–1877) of Dover and Dunkirk.

Rev Edward Horley (Rector 1883–1890) elder brother of Englebert.

THE BULCLEY CHANTRY

The earliest chantry (Bulcley) was founded about 1528 at an altar in the south-east chapel which indicates that the rebuilding was already complete by then.[9] An altar dedicated to Our Lady of Pity was set aside for '*an able and honest priest to say and celebrate mass and other divine service*' for Margaret Bulcley, her two husbands John Dutton and William Bulcley, and for others. She chose Robert Parkynson (aged about 42) during her lifetime and he was obliged to say '*Mass upon Saynt Margaretts day yerely for evir afore the ymage of Saynt Margaret within the said church*'. He was to have the ability to '*syng his playn song*' and '*to helpe to syng in the quere at Matyns, Masse, Evensong, and other dyvyne S'uye on festful days*'.[10] He was given a chalice weighing six ounces, a mass book and two vestments.

Margaret was the daughter of Sir Richard Molyneux (who died fighting for the Lancastrian cause at the Battle of Blore Heath 1459), the sister of James Molyneux, Rector here from 1489 and also Archdeacon of Richmond, and the aunt of Edward Molyneux B.D. This was the same Edward who became Rector in 1509 and left his own chantry.

At the chantry's dissolution in 1548, the plate and vestments disappeared, but the chantry priest, Robert Parkynson, received a pension for life of £4 6s out of its value of £4 14s.

BRASS OF MARGARET BULCLEY, 1528

Engraving of the Margaret Bulcley brass.

16 THE WORTHIES' WINDOW ERECTED BY RECTOR LONGFORD

Who were they?

Anthony Molineux T.D.

Born 1454, a Magdalen scholar and Fellow, described as a famous preacher in Henry VIII's time having been S.T.B. (D.D) in 1531. As Rector of Sefton Church he finished the building of the Chancel and built the vestry. He also endowed a school, formerly in the churchyard. He is thought to be buried in the chancel, '*my body to be buried at Sefton (yf I dept there) in the chauncell*'.[11]

William Warham 1450–1532

Originally a lawyer, he joined the Church and rose to become the Archbishop of Canterbury, who married and crowned Henry VIII and Catherine of Aragon. (wife number one). He was briefly Lord Chancellor but did not support the King in his quest to annul that marriage. He became very dispirited and afraid: 'The King's anger is death' he said and resigned to be succeeded by Wolsey.

Thomas Wolsey

Born 1473, a Magdalen scholar, ordained as a priest who in 1516 became a Cardinal of the Roman Church and Lord Chancellor. He was also Archbishop of York – in those days taking precedence over the Archbishop

Anthony Molyneux, Rector of Sefton.

of Canterbury. His home was Hampton Court Palace and he exercised considerable power and influence at Court and in the country. He fell out of favour with Henry VIII because he did not obtain from the Pope the annulment of the King's marriage to Catherine. Stripped of his power, his posts and his palace he was charged with treason and summonsed to London. He died before he could do so in 1530 to be succeeded by More.

Thomas More

Born 1478, lawyer, judge and in 1529 Lord Chancellor. He was a noted Oxford scholar; an author (he wrote *Utopia*); also a humanist, statesman and friend of Erasmus. By 1538, Anne Boleyn (wife number two) was pregnant (with Elizabeth I) although Henry VIII had not secured the annulment and More did not support the King. In 1534 Henry passed the Act of Supremacy, declaring himself Head of the Church in England (displacing the Pope) and annulled the marriage himself. He required all his subjects to take an Oath recognising Anne as his lawful wife (and any heir as lawful) and also his status as head of the English Church. More, along with John Fisher, Bishop of Rochester, refused to take the oath and both were

Sir Thomas More.

beheaded for treason in 1535. In 1935 they were both made Saints of the Roman Church.

John Colet 1467–1519

Scholar, humanist, Magdalen graduate, theologian, Dean of St Paul's London and founder of St Paul's school. He saw a great need for church reform (of the clergy in particular) and advocated clergy marriage. His teaching of the New Testament at Oxford was innovative for his time for Colet was against pomp and ceremony and placed great emphasis on humility, simple Christianity and the scriptures themselves.

The 'Worthies' Window.'

Richard Fox 1448–1528

Clergyman, politician and diplomat who rose to power in the reign of Henry VII. He arranged Prince Arthur's marriage to Catherine of Aragon. When Arthur died, Henry VIII (with a papal dispensation) married his sister-in-law. Eventually Fox became Archbishop of Winchester (the richest bishopric in England). With the rise of Wolsey he fell out of favour but survived with his wealth intact. His clothes and his very expensive bejewelled crosier (now in the Ashmolean Museum, Oxford) are pictured in the window. He founded Corpus Christi College Oxford – the first to provide for the teaching of Greek.

Thomas Linacre 1450–1524

Humanist, scholar, teacher and physician. His pupils included More, Erasmus, and Queen Mary I (Henry's daughter by Catherine). One of the first English scholars and teachers to study Classics abroad (Padua, Italy). He brought clerical scholarship back to Oxford.

William Grocyn 1449–1519

Cleric, Greek scholar, pupil of Linacre, one of the first to teach Greek at Oxford. He collected a formidable Latin and Greek library and his scholarly intellect was renowned by many including Erasmus.

What connects the 'Worthies' portrayed in the Window?

To begin with, all of them knew one another. Wareham was a particular friend of More, Colet, Linacre and Grocyn. Colet and More were personal friends, as was More of Henry VIII. Wolsey and More worked together in a political capacity as did Fox and Wolsey. Many were fellow scholars and Linacre's pupils. Moreover each 'worthy' featured would have been able to speak with first-hand knowledge, experience and authority as to the religious and political events concerning 'The Reformation', the personalities involved and the dilemmas and choices facing those in power and influence both in the Church and State. Anthony Molineux was Rector of Sefton Church during this period.

For Rector Longford, however, a Magdalen scholar, the significance of the early sixteenth-century men depicted in our window was that they were leaders in the New Learning which was to overthrow many of the errors of medieval religion and to 'reform its practices'. Wareham he describes as a 'great friend of the New Learning'. Fox founded Corpus Christi College which taught Greek; Wolsey founded Christ Church Oxford for the pursuit of the New (and reformative) religious learning. Sir Thomas More wrote *Utopia* in 1516, a controversial work concerning an imaginary island where there was religious tolerance, communal ownership, men and women educated alike, and no lawyers! Colet, Linacre and Grocyn were 'academics' and supporters of a new philosophical and reformative approach in religious teaching.

And thus, Rector Longford (who put great a deal of time and his own money into Sefton Church) provides us with a deeper and more insightful meaning into the word 'Reformation' than the drama and controversy portrayed in films, TV programmes and books. . . . A Re-Formation in fact of what had gone before. (Courtesy of H. H. Judith Daley).

17 MORTUARY SLAB

RECTORS OF SEFTON

1204	RICHARD MOLYNEUX[12]
1206	ROBERT
1288	WILLIAM DE KIRKDALE
1310	RICHARD DE MOLYNEUX[13]
1339	GILBERT DE LEGH
1339	JOHN DE MASCY
1364	JORDAN DE HOLME, A.M.[14]
1376	WILLIAM DE OKE
1378	SIMON DE MELBURN
1404	ROGER HAWKSHAW
1416	JOHN TOTTY
1427	RICHARD DE HAYDOCK
1432	NICHOLAS DE HAYDOCK
1433	RICHARD DEL KAR
1462	JOHN MOLYNEUX, A.M.[15]
1485	HENRY MOLYNEUX, A.M.
1489	JAMES MOLYNEUX
1509	EDWARD MOLYNEUX, S.T.B.[16]

The mortuary slab inscribed with the List of Rectors behind the Robert Thompson table.

1535	ANTHONY MOLYNEUX, S.T.D.[17]
1557	ROBERT BALLARD
1564	JOHN FINCH[18]
1567	JOHN NUTTER, B.D.[19]
1601	GREGORY TURNER, M.A.
1633	THOMAS LEGH, D.D.
1639	EDWARD MORTON, D.D.
c.1646	JOSEPH THOMSON[20] (no legal title)
1660	EDWARD MORTON D.D.
1675	JOHN BRADFORD, D.D. (Double presentation. Bradford called 'ex chaplain in ordinary'. Swapped Living of Bexhill with his successor, Brideoak)
1678	JONATHAN BRIDEOAK, B.D.
1684	RICHARD RICHMOND, M.A.
1722	THOMAS EGERTON, M.A.
1763	RICHARD ROTHWELL, M.A.
1801	RICHARD RAINSHAW ROTHWELL, M.A.
1863	ROGER DAWSON-DUFFIELD, LL.D. (Count Dawson-Duffield)
1871	ENGELBERT HORLEY, M.A.
1883	EDWARD HORLEY, M.A.
1890	GEORGE WILLIAM WALL, M.A.
1907	HERBERT METHUEN WELLS, M.A.
1932	W. W. LONGFORD, D.D.
1961	F. T. BARNSLEY WEBBER, M.A.
1969	GEORGE O. FARRAN, M.A.
1973	OWEN JAMES YANDEL, M.A.
1992	PATRICK JOHN CREAN, M.A.
1998	IRENE CHRISTINE COWELL
2013	NICOLA MILFORD, B.Th.

12 THE ROTHWELL CONNECTION

Visitors to Sefton cannot avoid noticing the name Rothwell. The family held the Advowson for over two hundred years, and provided two Rectors of Sefton, as well as embellishing the church and rectory.

The Rothwells originated in Lancashire, and it is possible that one William Rothwell, who was Vicar of Deane 1541–1563 and a Chaplain to Henry VIII, was related to our Sefton rectors.

What is extraordinary is how members of this Lancashire family became Counts of Sardinia and Marquises of Monaco, as well as bosom friends of the President of the Confederate States of America. The latter, Mr Jefferson Davies and his wife were once entertained at Sefton Rectory by the Curate in Charge, Rev John Cumming MacDona. They were amazed to see six dogs, each with a monkey on its back which the curate had trained to run in a steeplechase.

Rector Richard Rainshaw Rothwell
(Rector 1801–1863).

James Rothwell was born into a prosperous family and went up to Brasenose College, Oxford where he obtained his B.A. degree in 1711, aged twenty-three. When he married Sarah Rainshaw of Manchester in 1718, his family fortunes increased. The name of Rainshaw lives on to this day, in the personage of Christopher Rainshaw Rothwell of Lulworth who has kindly sponsored this book. James was another Rothwell Vicar of Deane, and wealthy enough to purchase the Advowson of Sefton, which in the mid-nineteenth century was to become the second richest in the country. This gave him the right to appoint Rectors. James, although buried in Deane Church, is commemorated on the Rothwell Monument at Sefton.

Although strange to us now, parish rectors were then not obliged to be present in their livings: it was usual to employ curates to administer the sacraments and provide pastoral care. On the death of Rev Thomas Egerton in 1763, James appointed his son, Rev Richard Rothwell to the benefice. Richard was an absentee Rector, living mainly at Sharples Hall, and when he died he was buried at Deane rather than Sefton.

Rector Rothwell's signature.

Richard's eldest son James (1765–1824) became Lord of the Manor of Much Hoole; his third son Ralph (1776–1824) lived at Ribbleton Hall, Preston and had issue, while his second son and namesake inherited the Advowson and effectively appointed himself as Rector of Sefton.

Rev Richard Rainshaw Rothwell (1771–1863) was a bachelor, and his domestic arrangements were a mirror image of those of his late father: he lived at Sefton but maintained Sharples Hall. He retained five outdoor and five indoor servants while his married curate with five children lived in Lunt House with one servant.

Rector Rothwell was also a Chaplain to Lord Palmerston, Prime Minister, which placed remote little Sefton surprisingly at the heart of the British establishment. Rector Rothwell became a wealthy man, leaving an enormous estate of £160,000 on his death aged 92 in 1863. He left the bulk of his estate to the four children of his brother Ralph (died 1821) of Ribbleton Hall, Preston. The eldest, another Richard Rainshaw Rothwell (1809–1890) received the Advowson. It was he who was later destined to become a Count and a Marquis.

It is remarkable that a father and son held the Rectory of Sefton for 100 years.

Richard Rainshaw Rothwell moved in international circles and Liverpool placed him in a sphere of great influence. He was friendly with the Count de Sallon, uncle of Count Cavour, the Prime Minister of Piedmont and it is possible that Cavour had met Rothwell at Sharples Hall, Tatton Park, or even Sefton Rectory as it is known that he visited Liverpool. Rothwell was obviously moved by the chaos and poverty he heard about and, among other things, he donated the handsome sum of £2000 to an eye hospital in Sardinia. His empathy and practical efforts were much appreciated and he was created a Count of Sardinia. Modern visitors to Rome will be familiar with Cavour Metro Station on Via Cavour.

After the famous Treaty of Vienna (1815), Napoleon's unification of Italian states was dismembered, with Monaco returned from France to the Kingdom of Piedmont Sardinia. There was a people's movement in Italy, led by Mazzini and Garibaldi, and supported in this country mainly by liberals, to agitate for a united Kingdom of Italy. There were serious riots in Birkenhead in October 1860 by ultramontanists when Garibaldi was invited to speak in the town. The vicar, whose church hall was chosen to host the event was known to be an Orangeman and the posters advertising it were printed in orange ink. Fifty-five policemen were

View of the chancel, looking west, by Richard Bridgens 1822.

injured in the mêlée, thirteen seriously. Liverpool, however, became a key player, sending supplies and volunteers to support the guerrilla forces. The S.S. *Queen of England* sailed from Liverpool on 2nd August 1860 with warlike stores and on 22nd September 1860 about 80 volunteers left the port to join guerrilla forces in Naples. The exact nature of Rothwell's involvement is not known, but he obviously gave assistance behind the scenes. Having access through his nephew to Lord Palmerston, the Prime Minister, was obviously most useful and he certainly found favour with a grateful Charles III, the Prince of Monaco.

Monaco was returned to France and Italy unified once again in 1861. Garibaldi was fêted in England three years later when Queen Victoria was displeased that more people turned out for him than for her. For his efforts, Rothwell, who had already been made a Count of Sardinia, was further ennobled by being made an hereditary Marquis of Monaco. Mr Christopher Rainshaw Rothwell of Lulworth is the 5th Marquis although he does not normally use the title.

Rev Richard Rainshaw Rothwell (Rector of Sefton 1801–1863)

To hold a living for 62 years was a great achievement in those days – as it still would be today.

Owning the Advowson himself, he was very much the King of the Parish, but a kind and benevolent one at that. He took scant notice of his Bishop (of Chester), and ran the church to his own liking. He was a scholar and a gentleman who took a personal interest in physical as well as spiritual health. He frequently walked the four miles or so to the coast to bathe – even in winter, and encouraged sports and physical exercises in the village.

He was an aesthete, an expert on Shakespeare and an avid theatre-goer. It is said that as he mowed his own field, he practised his skill in oratory.

A letter from Liverpool, signed by *An Admirer of our Inimitable Prayer Book,* written on Monday 20th August 1849 states that on first hearing Rev Richard Rainshaw Rothwell his,

'*. . . expectation had been raised to the utmost stretch, yet like the Queen of Sheba, it far exceeded all that I heard*'.

Also another witness, Rev T. Briarly Browne of East Acklam, York, who had known the Rector from boyhood, wrote about him being, '*kind and humane . . . and always ready to help the poor*'. He cites a period when several, '*necessitous persons, among others an old man – Dennis Halliwell – who was a Roman Catholic*' boarded and lodged in the Rectory. He was obviously practising what he preached, and after his death he was long and fondly remembered.

The sacred monogram on the reredos.

0 THE CHANDELIERS

We are fortunate to possess three large, brass, twelve-branch chandeliers dating from 1773. Little is known of their fabrication or history but we do know that the church accounts show a payment of 2/- in 1820 for *Carting Chandeliers from Canal* and in 1826 21/- was paid for *Gilding Doves on Chandeliers*. The doves themselves are interesting. Made of wood and gilded, they show the birds in flight, very similar to a silver dove in the Metropolitan Museum in New York. There the dove is from Byzantium, Attarouthi in Syria and dated to the sixth–seventh century. It originally held a cross in its mouth, with its legs tucked away under its body as if in flight. The dove symbolised the Holy Spirit appearing over Christ's head at his baptism by John the Baptist, as told by Matthew 3:16.

In a smoky, dusty environment the brass probably needed a good clean every fifty years or so and would be shipped into Liverpool down the canal. Now they are lacquered and in pristine condition and probably look exactly like they did in 1773.

Fortunately, as electricity only came to Sefton Church in the early 1970s, the chandeliers were never converted, but always used for their original purpose – to shed light from real candles. Now we have the luxury of lighting them for special events such as the midnight Eucharist at Christmas when they lend a mellow glow in an age of fluorescent tubing.

Let them remind us that Jesus is the Light of the World.

Inscriptions:

Two of the chandeliers (currently the east and west ones) bear the same inscription:
Rich.d. Rothwell A.M. Rector & Patron
John Whalley
Rich.d. Goore Church Wardens

The middle chandelier is inscribed:
The Gift of Rich.d. Rothwell
Rector & Patron
1773

The chandeliers were cleaned and restored in 1995 by the generosity of E. Mary Jackson.

Chandeliers.

Plate

The church plate consists of a chalice with the letters and the inscription '*The gift of Mrs. Alice Morton to the church of Sephton, 1695*'; a flagon, inscribed '*The gift of Mrs. Anne Jackson of Sephton, 1715*'; another chalice, *with* '*The gift of Mrs. Ann Molyneux to the parish church of Sephton, 1729*', and among the plate marks B.B. for Benjamin Branker, a Liverpool silversmith; a cylindrical cup with handle, engraved with a crest of three arrows, tied with ribbon, and the points resting on a wreath; and a silver paten, which fits an old silver chalice given to St Luke's, Great Crosby. The Sefton Plate is now kept in secure vaults.

The Parish Registers

Parish Registers were first introduced by Cardinal Ximenes in Toledo in 1497, then later in western Europe. In England, after the Reformation, they were instigated in 1538, although they were often neglected because they were thought to be part of a new tax system.

They provide a rich social history and deserve a volume in their own right. Sefton's earliest registers are kept in temperature controlled conditions in Preston, although they have also been published by the Lancashire and Cheshire Historical Society, Volume 86.

Sefton Plate, consisting of a large silver plate given by Mrs Ann Jackson and Mrs Alice Morton in 1695, a large wine flagon presented by Mrs Anne Jackson in 1715, and a large communion cup given by Mrs Ann Molyneux in 1729.

They start as follows:

Baptizati (Baptisms)	February 7 1597
Connubia (Marriages)	July 21 1600
Sepulti (Burials)	July 13 1600
Churchings	after 1617

There are gaps in the registers – some explained, but others not. There are no baptisms 1605–1614; no marriages 1603–1615; and no burials 1605–1613.

During the Civil Wars, we find the following note in the Baptisms for 1644: '*The warrs being greevous in the cuntrie both regesters and others were neglected til . . .*' (July 16).

In 1641 and 1642 there was only one marriage listed each year, and in 1643 and 1644 there were no marriages but the word '*Warr*' is written opposite the dates.

In 1646 and 1647, we find '*none made by the minister*' and in 1648 we read a little more:

'*None married by the minister of the Parish, Jos: Thompson, Rector*'.

Not only was the war political but it was also religious. At the Reformation, Catholic clergy were put out of their Livings, but a century later, Anglicans were also ousted – this time in favour of Presbyterians such as Jos Thompson. Joseph Thompson, in fact, had no legal title to the Living.

One plausible reason for the marriages' issue is that couples from Sefton might have gone to Everton Beacon (250 feet above sea level) to be married by their old priest Edward Morton who had been ousted, or to Sefton Hall Chapel.

Everton was the hilltop village where Prince Rupert of the Rhine spied on Liverpool Town before recapturing it for the Royalist cause. The Beacon was in communication with Beeston Castle in Cheshire, and with Billinge, Ashurst and Rivington.

Morton reappears in the registers in 1662 although Thompson must have been a capable and agreeable man as he continues to take at least an administrative role in the parish for a period after this time. He was said by the Parliamentary Commissioners to be 'an able and godly minister, painfull in his cure'.[21]

A wedding at Sefton in the early nineteenth century.

In 1649 we find only one marriage and between 1650–1652 there are '*none married by the minister*'. For the years 1653–1656 we have a change, as the new Commonwealth introduced Civil Marriages.

'*All marriages made by the Justice of the Peace*'. Then in 1657, a note: '*That act of marrying by Justices was to continue but six months after the first session of the Pliamt (parliament) ended in December*'.

Burials

Burials get omitted from the registers in 1645: '*A time of warr neglected*' and in 1646, '*A time of warr noethinge found*'.

The Parish Hearse

A parish hearse (maybe that of 1714) first appears in the Church Wardens' Accounts in 1751 where we see, *Rec. for the Hearse 13/-*. Horses to pull the hearse might have been engaged separately, or maybe it was driven by manpower. In the following decades, there are constant references to repairs and refurbishments, and little income recorded. By 1866 it needed replacing and a new one, with four plumes, was purchased for £104. Only five years later in 1871, with an annual income that year of only 3/6, the hearse disappears from the parish accounts. Probably after that time, it was provided free and maintained by private individuals, before it disappeared completely.

It is interesting that on the odd occasion in the twenty-first century, we see plumed horses drawing an elaborate antique hearse up to the lych gate.

Church Briefs

Everton Beacon – now the site of St George's Church. It is thought that many Sefton weddings took place in this royalist stronghold during the Civil War.

The registers also list Church Briefs, which were collections ordered by the Crown for other towns which were suffering from some disaster such as plague or fire. Grantham, Weedon, Flackborow, Sandwich, Tynmouth, Southampton, Southwark and Wem were among the many places which benefitted from Sefton's generosity.

Catholics

After the Reformation, Catholics still needed to get baptised, married and buried. Apart from problems at Sefton around 1611–1620 when the Parson refused to bury Catholics in the Churchyard, the old and new dispensations lived reasonably peacefully side by side. The Lords of the Manors of Sefton, Little Crosby and Ince were all Catholics and afforded a large degree of protection to their tenantry.

According to the Rev'd T. E. Gibson, in Lancashire some children were baptised twice – once by the established church then secondly by 'massing priests'. It was also common for Catholic funeral rites to be performed at home before going to the church: some mourners buried the deceased themselves while others entreated the parson to omit the funeral service. Others left the church when the parson read the service, or kneeling around the body, said their own private prayers neglecting the public service.

Cathedralesque proportions of Sefton Church.

Recusants '*refuse not to bring it* (the corpse) *to the Churche, thoughe they will not partake of the service of the Churche*'.

It is only in the early eighteenth century, as a result of panic caused by the Jacobite Rebellions, that the word '*papist*' appears in the registers. The first such entry is:

'*1706 Nov 6 Richard s(on) John Sutton papist de Sefton*'.

After that we frequently find Catholics being baptised and listed as 'papists'. Names such as Mercer, Harrison, Blundell, Travers, Lydiate, Houghton, Gilbertson, Hunt, Darwin, Newhouse, Litherland, Thorpe, Fairclough, Tristram, Plumbe, Hyton, Fleetwood and Cokshut fill the pages.

The Mersey Estuary could be perilous: 'Rock-Point' near Liverpool (now New Brighton). *Courtesy of E. J. Crighton.*

Drowning

The Crosby coast was treacherous at times and any bodies washed up were laid out on the mortuary slab at the Church Inn next to Sefton Church before burial (the slab is now in the church and inscribed with the list of Rectors of Sefton).

16th February 1742 we find,

'*John Fatherley distressed at Sea died in Great Crosby buried here an Irishman and his wife both sailing thither*'.

13th September 1762 we read *'James Noise found upon Crosby shore Born at Bristol buried here'*. On 22nd September 1762, *'James Oil thrown upon Gt. Crosby Shore buried here'*.

16th September 1777, *'A woman unknown cast upon Gt. Crosby Shore'* and on 22nd of the same month, another.

A Priest

On 20th April 1746 we find the burial of a Catholic Priest who was attached to the Molyneux Family: *'Mr Kendal, Priest from Crocksteth'*.

SADLER FAMILY GRAVES

In the angle between the chancel and the south aisle lie the two original Sadler gravestones whose text is now almost illegible. They are inscribed as follows:

> *Here lies the Body*
> *of Elizabeth Sadler*
> *wife of Adam Sadler*
> *who departed this life*
> *the 10th of May 1760*
> *aged 87.*

> *Here lieth the body of John Adam*
> *Sadler Lieut in the Royal Navy*
> *who departed this life 30th Jany*
> *1816 aged 37 years.*
> *May he rest in peace.*

> *Here are deposited the remains*
> *of the Revd James Parker Catholic*
> *Priest who departed this life on the*
> *29th day of October 1822 in the 75th*
> *Year of his age.*
> *Requiscant in pace* (sic)
> *No more to be interred in this grave.*

> *Here lies the body*
> *of Adam Sadler who*
> *departed this Life*
> *the 7th of October 1765*
> *aged 83.*

> *Here also lies the Body of Mr*
> *John Sadler from Liverpool who*
> *departed this life the 10th of*
> *December 1789 aged 69.*

Here also lies the body of James
son of the said Mr John Sadler
who departed this Life the 27th
of December 1794 aged 8½ years.

Also the body of Elizabeth widow of
Mr John Sadler who departed this life
the 25th of May 1842 aged 88 years.

Also of Elizabeth Mary Sadler
of Aintree Daughter of the above
who departed this life the 19th of
June 1857 aged 75 years.
Requiescant in Pace.
No more to be buried in this grave.

The new stone reads as follows:

John Sadler 1720–1789
Son of Adam
Buried here
The inventor with Guy Green
of Transfer Printing onto
Pottery which revolutionised
The World Industry.

Liverpool Pottery and the Sefton Shore

The history of pottery in Liverpool is obscure, although an early written record in the list of town dues is dated 1674.[22] It contains the following items: '*For every cart-load of mugs (shipped) into foreign ports, 6d.; for every cartload of mugs along the coasts, 4d.; for every crate of cupps or pipes along the coast, 1d*'. By 1790, the pottery industry employed 374 people in the town.

A famous delftware plaque entitled *A West Prospect of Great Crosby 1716* (unfortunately destroyed during the blitz on the Liverpool Museum) not only gives us a very early date for

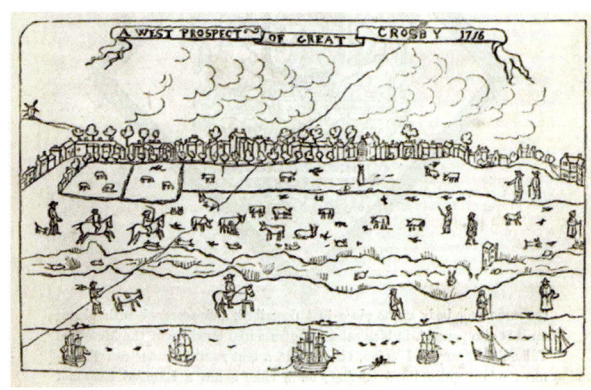

A West Prospect of Great Crosby 1716.
Made in Liverpool, this early deftware plaque was destroyed by enemy bombing.

Liverpool pottery, but also a tantalising view of the layers of water and land use. First of all there is the river with a range of vessels in sail, including a large boat with a smaller one attached to its stern. There is also a small boat with two men in it rowing towards her. There are various gulls and aquatic birds around the boats.

The sands provide the first road, with a man driving an ass, a man on horseback and people walking, two with baskets. Above them is the rabbit warren in the sand dunes, and a small house for the keeper of the warren; then men, two on horseback, with cows, birds and a dog. A large area at the back is divided into larger and smaller plots with hedgerows. They hold cattle, a milkmaid carrying a pail on her head and two men seemingly conversing as they stroll along. In the background is the town with its long rows of houses, the school house, and many trees. On the far left is the windmill, which still exists. The plaque was thought to have been made in the works of Alderman Shaw, situated at the bottom of Dale Street.

Fortunately, a drawing survives of the plaque which was cracked long before it was destroyed (illustrated above).

Mr Adam Sadler of Aintry (Aintree) 1682–9th October 1765

Adam Sadler became a printer and engraver in Liverpool but also engraved silver tobacco boxes and household items. As a young man he was a favourite soldier of the Duke of Marlborough in the wars in the Low Countries and it was there whilst lodging in the house of a printer that he gained an insight into the trade. On the accession of George I, he could not support the Brunswicks and left the army in disgust, forfeiting all his arrears in pay. Retiring to Ulverston, he married a Miss Bibby who was acquainted with two of the daughters of the Lord of Sefton, and through their influence, moved firstly to Melling, then to a house and farm at Aintree. His lease, of 1723, was *made between the Right Hon. Sir Richard Molyneux, Bart., Lord Viscount Molyneux of Maryburgh, in the Kingdom of Ireland, on the one part, and Adam Sadler, of Melling, gentleman, on the other part*.

Detail of a printed tile by Sadler and Green.

He became a successful businessman as a printer in the New Market in Liverpool, where he produced a large number of books including 'The Muse's Delight' – a comprehensive collection of songs with music. He was an accomplished musician himself with the violin being his favourite instrument. He took an apprentice, Guy Green, who succeeded him to the business and later went into partnership with Adam's son, John.

John Sadler (1720–1789)

There was obviously a close personal relationship between the Sadlers and the Greens as Guy and his wife Jane were the Godparents of John and Elizabeth's son John when he was baptised at Gillmoss Catholic Chapel (St Swithin's) in 1778. John (junior) was buried at Gillmoss on 18th April 1816. James, another son, was born in 1786 and *casually drowned in the canal at Aintree* in 1794 before being buried at Sefton.

John bought a house from his father in Harrington Street for the nominal sum of 5s and set up business there in 1748. He married Elizabeth Parker whose father was a watchmaker of Seel Street and uncle, a Mr Fazackerly, a silversmith of Pool Lane. It is said that he was so successful that other townsfolk became jealous of him and persuaded the corporation to remove him as he was not a freeman of the town. Among other things he was accused of being the publisher of '*a most scandalous paper lately printed at Liverpoole ...*'. This hyperbole probably sprang from a political controversy. He also published a fine engraving of Sefton Church in 1752: '*The South-East Prospect of Sefton Church in Lancashire*' which unfortunately perpetuated the idea of its foundation in AD IIII.

He won his case against the town council and is credited for an influx of business people who flocked into the booming borough to find their fortunes.

He later became interested in printing on pottery after watching children sticking waste prints to pieces of broken pottery. He secretly made many experiments before sharing his ideas with Guy Green. The two prepared all the paperwork in order to secure a Patent from the King, but decided that it was unnecessary. They are generally credited as being the discoverers of a method of printing on pottery from copper plates (previously all decoration was hand painted).

On a sworn affidavit of 1756, Sadler and Guy Green stated that '*without the aid or assistance of any person or persons, (they) did, (on 27th July) within the space of six hours, to wit, betwixt the hours of nine in the morning and three in the afternoon of the same day, print upwards of twelve hundred earthenware tiles of different patterns, at Liverpoole (sic) aforesaid, and which as these depondents have heard and believe, were more in number and better and neater, than one hundred skilful pot painters could have painted in the like space of time in the common and usual way*'.[23]

This was confirmed on 2nd August 1756 by two local worthies, Thomas Shaw and Samuel Gilbody, who further stated that Sadler and Green had, '*been several years in bringing the art of printing on earthenware to perfection*' and they had

Royal Souvenir of the Golden Jubilee 1897 made for the Parish of Sefton.

'never heard it was done by any other person or persons but themselves'. Later that month, on the 13th, Ellis Cunliffe, Spencer Steers and Charles Goore added their own imprimatur.

Early signed examples of copper plate engravings are a portrait of Frederick III, King of Prussia (after an original painted in Berlin in 1756), a portrait of George II, a quart mug with a well executed landscape, a teapot with the crest of the Earl of Derby and a legend, and a number of square tiles (see illustration).

Josiah Wedgwood, after perfecting his famous 'Queen's Ware' pottery, went into a business partnership with Sadler and Green, sending blanks to Liverpool for printing. Finished wares were either exported immediately by sea (with large numbers going to America), or sent back to Etruria in Staffordshire. There are invoices from Guy Green as late as 1794 confirming these arrangements.

Elizabeth Mary Sadler (1782–1857)

John and Elizabeth's only daughter, also called Elizabeth, lived to the ripe old age of 75 in Aintree Lane, and died in June 1857. The entry in the register at Sefton lists her as 'Romanist'.

Richard Abbey lived at Abbey's Farm, (where the Holy Rosary Church now stands). He was an apprentice to John Sadler in 1767. Richard went on to open the first pottery on the Herculaneum site in South Liverpool, about 1794, where he created a famous set of tiles depicting Aesop's Fables. Both Sadler and Abbey have pottery on display in Liverpool Museum. Many pottery sites and potters followed in the Liverpool area.

Hanged and Buried

Perhaps the most unusual entry in the registers appears in 1652:

> *'Aug 6 Anne Rothwell wid(ow) of Much Crosby hanged and buryed'*.

Whether she hanged herself or was the victim of the Witchfinder General, we are unsure.

Good Friday at Sefton.

Some interesting Deaths

1650 March 12	Robart Lunt of Luntt, old man
1651 August 27	Shurlaretto d(aughter) Rich: Mollinex of Netherton.
1654 Sept 18	Winefrid Smith a little wench of Greate Crosbee, d(aughter) to Rothwell's brother
1772 July 16	Edwd Rigby alias Peel

1773 April 6   Mary Bushel of Ince sd to be above 100 years old.

1773 Aug 18   Thos Johnson a Nurse-child from Robt Mellings of Thornton.

Local Gentry

The burials of the Molyneux Family and the Blundells of Crosby and Ince are also recorded.

Church Wardens' Accounts

Up to about 1834, the Church was responsible for much of the local government in the Parish. The Parish Constables at Sefton were also the Overseers of the Poor and it is pleasing to note their generosity.

1719   *Given to 2 Travileing ffrench mariners 6d.*

1749   Jan. 16th – grants given to a *'company of Salors'*, a man who had lost cattle, and a man who viewed windows for the window tax.

      'Several Sealors yt had be ill Abused with Turks', boys for catching 96 sparrows, a man who had lost everything in a fire, several men with a pass (a sort of passport for travelling through various parishes), and a *'Souldier going to his own country'*.

One of the most unusual grants was, *'Gave Thos ffairclough to pay for part of his wives coffin 3s 9d'*. One wonders if he had several wives to bury at once or if his wife had only a partial coffin.

In 1725 the stocks had to be renewed (and again in 1791). These are probably the Stocks which can be seen in Thornton today by the Cross. We know that a man was put in the Stocks in 1863 on the authority of the Marquis de Rothwell.

In 1728 the Ducking Stool and Pinfold had to be repaired. In Saxon times known as a *'scealfing-stole'*, one was in use in Liverpool until 1779. The Pinfold/ Pound (Saxon = *pinden, to shut up*) was in Brickwall Lane.

The Dog-Whipper was appointed up to 1820. His duties (salary 1770 = 5s/1807 = 10s), was to keep dogs out of church during services and sometimes to waken up members of the congregation who were snoring heavily during sermons.

We are not sure of the existence of a Town Crier or Bellman, although these costs appear as follows:

1725   *Spent at making Uan Cry 6d.*

1726   *Spent at making Uwan Cry for Ja:Bibye, 6d.*

Is that *'Hue & Cry?'*

A Scarecrow features in 1789: *'Shoeing the Crow, 1s'.*

The greatest expenses by far were always connected with victuals at the Punch Bowl Inn next door (Ellen/Nelly Barker's) at Easter, Court and sundry days. The Church Wardens liberally treated themselves as in 1751 when they 'spent on ourselves' 'when the writings were laid up in the chest' and in 1752 'spent when agreed what to give towards propagating the Gospel in forreign parts' and in 1759 when they celebrated the 'taking of Quebec'. Occasionally they 'spent on ourselves and some of the Parish', especially on 5th November which was the parish feast day when enormous sums were paid for victuals (£3 3s.7d. in 1810).

One strange entry occurs in 1781 when they sent their, 'Expenses to Liverpool with a Bill of Damage in the Vestry, done by the Press-Gang', and another in 1811 when a sum of money was paid for, 'shot and powder for the use of the church'. There are frequent references to 'cleaning S. Helen's Well' for which the children were given 5s. after they had said the catechism.

The Jubilee of George III in 1809 involved serious money:

'*To the Jubilee £24 9s 2d*', then another '£10 11s 4d'. 'Court Fees and Form of Prayer 12s 2d;' 'spent on the *Duble* (Jubilee) *Day, 9s*'.

A year later, the Church still owed money for the celebrations:

'*1811–arrears – October 25, to the Jubilee Day – £1 2s 9d*'.

A brief Historical and Descriptive Account of Sefton Church, by Richard Bridgens, London 1822.

Because of its antiquity and singular beauty, Sefton Church has attracted much attention in the past. One of the most extraordinary visual accounts of it is to be found in a large folio volume published by Richard Bridgens in London. He was an architect by profession and living in Liverpool at the time. The church is proud to possess a copy which is displayed in a special bookcase near the lectern.

Containing but few words, it is full of architectural-style drawings which can be compared with details as we find them today.

It is an enjoyable survey of the building as he found it in 1818 – just before some important changes took place. It ends with a romantic notion of the church lying in ruins with two knights in armour looking down on one of the stone effigies – something which appealed to the Georgian psyche. In the sixteenth and seventeenth centuries, our forefathers gazed upon the ruins of our great abbeys and priories, probably with dismay and regret. By the eighteenth century, they almost found a virtue in broken masonry now covered with vegetation. It is amusing, but also a provocative warning of the future.

We must also test his other illustrations against reality. His drawing of the south elevation of the building is out of proportion. His ground plan is missing certain essential features, the font is too squat, a Molyneux Brass occupies a different position and shows three extra children, and an arched window has become square-headed. All this is most decorative, but we must exercise extreme caution and treat it as a romanticised version of Sefton Church.

William Douglas Caröe 1857–1938. The 'Golden Stain of Time' in Sefton Church

Despite becoming an architect of great renown, responsible for the cathedrals of St David's and Durham and the abbeys of Tewksbury and Romney, W. D. Caröe preferred Sefton Church to them all, including St Paul's Cathedral. In Liverpool, he is usually remembered for his imaginative Gustav Adolf Church (1884) in Park Lane, an octagonal ensemble in red brick with a roof of tiles and copper surmounted by a leaden spire. For a young man in his twenties, this was a remarkable achievement.

The son of the Danish Consul in Liverpool, he went up to Trinity College Cambridge (graduating in 1879) before launching his own practice in 1884 as Caröe & Partners. No doubt his father helped him gain the Liverpool commission, but he had been articled to John Loughborough Pearson, a leading ecclesiastical architect of the day.

Unlike many Victorian 'Church Restorers', he believed in retaining ancient features in churches, which might seem inconvenient or old-fashioned to others. He despised repairs which had been undertaken with *'laudably conservative intentions, but completed to fulfil those curious conditions with which modern church worship seems prone to surround itself, a drawing-room neatness and ultra-propriety of style – a quite classic precision, decked in a pseudo-Gothic garb, insipidity deep-woven into its texture'*.

With his sister-in-law, Eleanor Jane Alexandra Caröe (1863–1913), he wrote 'SEFTON A Descriptive and Historical Account' in 1893, into which he incorporated the research and notes of Rev Englebert Horley, M.A. (Rector 1871–1883), and the complete, then extant records of the Mock Corporation. Your scribe is lucky to possess Eleanor's own personal copy and he is indebted to the authors for their painstaking scholarship and labour.

Caröe was entrusted with the job of making the church 'stable', and removing 'unsightly excrescences' such as the white washing on the walls, the clumsy Georgian box pews and cluttered galleries, and replacing the painted deal roofs. He promised to exercise a 'restraining hand' on certain items, such as the classical reredos and the Mock Corporation pew – features in 'dubious harmony' yet of real historic interest.

To complete the work and raise the final £2000 out of the total cost of £5000, a Grand Bazaar was held over three days, 25th–27th April 1912, at the Alexandra

Hall in Blundellsands with a Season Ticket costing 2/6. The Countess of Sefton, The Hon. Arthur Stanley, MP and Mrs Chavasse (wife of the bishop) opened the fair on successive days and by all accounts it was a grand affair with something for everyone. You could buy curtains and cushions made on the only handloom in Liverpool, cigars, cigarettes, ash trays and pipes. There were also exotic mandarins and orange blossom direct from Nice, as well as nurses' caps and aprons (for children). Presents could be wrapped (for a small fee) and they could be delivered in the neighbourhood for 3d each from its own post office.

There were also competitions, such as composing the best sentence from the letters in the following words: 'The Village Fair is in aid of Sefton Church Restoration', with a first prize of a handsome 10/-. In the afternoons and evenings there were musical and theatrical performances with a Mrs Sauze and a Captain Becher apparently leading the way. It must have been an exciting and profitable adventure.

Curious alms box, designed by Caröe.

The River Mersey today.

1 2nd Lt Richard Shirburne Weld-Blundell (born 1887) died after an accidental fall at Ramsgate, 1st January 1916. Buried Ince Blundell. Louis Joseph Weld-Blundell (born 1889) died of influenza while on active service, 8th February 1919, Dunkirk). Buried Dunkirk Town Cemetery.

2 St Ambrose, *Oratio de obitu Theodosii*.

3 Eusebius, *Vita Constantini, III, xlvii*.

4 William D. Caröe, *Sefton A Descriptive and Historical Account*, (London, Longmans, Green, and Co. 1893).

5 Dorning Rasbotham (1730–1791) son of Peter Rasbotham was born in Manchester. His mother was Hannah, daughter of John Dorning of Farnworth in the parish of Dean (where James Rothwell was the rector). He made extensive collections for a history of Lancashire which Baines used in his own History of Lancashire.

6 Trans. Frank Tyrer, The Great Diurnal of Nicholas Blundell of Little Crosby, Lancashire, Volume Two 1712–1719, (The Record Society of Lancashire and Cheshire)

7 *The Illustrated Itinerary of the County of Lancashire*, (London, How and Parsons, 1842).

8 Raines's Lanc. Chantries, xxvii, and 113.

9 See Bulcley Chantry – page 31.

10 Margaret Bulcley's Will was made on 4th November 1528.

11 Will of Anthony Molyneux, reprinted in Caröe.

12 Precise dates of early rectors are difficult to define as often we only have documents which mention them as 'parson of Sefton' when already in post. To add more mystery, there is a Richard mentioned in 1224 and another Richard in 1281.

13 – He was in court with two others charged with taking a buck at Aykeberewe (Aigburth?) 28 Sept 1322. Cited in *South Lancashire in the reign of Edward II AS ILLUSTRATED BY THE PLEAS AT WIGAN RECORDEDI IN CORAM REGE ROLL NO. 254* p. 102 Manchester University Press.

14 Jordan de Holme was previously Rector of Stockport and became Rector here by exchange.

15 John Molyneux was the uncle of Margaret Bulcley, and also a Prebendary of Lichfield Cathedral.

16 Edward Molyneux was also Prebendary of Farndon, Sarum. He was renowned as litigious and thoroughly unpleasant. Maybe he was hoping to knock off some years in purgatory by founding the Molyneux (or Mollinex) Chantry at Sefton.

17 Anthony Molyneux certainly built the Revestry and maybe completed the rebuilding of the church. He was also Rector of Walton (Liverpool was a Chapelry in that parish). He resigned in 1557 and died in 1558.

18 John Finch was a priest at Walton and paid 'first fruits' at Sefton on 23rd November 1564.

19 John Nutter was the notorious 'pluralist' – holding the Rectories of Sefton, Bebington and Aughton. He was also Dean of Chester in 1589 and set about to promote 'the race of the Gospel' by getting rid of Catholics, in particular by attacking the Blundell family. He did show kindness once by pleading, together with Sir Richard Molyneux, for the release of Mrs Emilia Blundell who was in Chester Gaol for her '*uncomformitie, obstinacie and disobedience*' in religion. As the Crosby Records note, the qualifications of Molyneux for promoting the new religion were dubious, as a marginal note attached to his name states that he, '*maketh shew of good conformitie, but many of his companie are in evill note*'. Enormously wealthy, Queen Elizabeth I possibly borrowed from Apuleius the title of 'The Golden Ass' which she bestowed upon him on account of his wealth. When he died, bags of gold were discovered under his bed in Sefton Rectory.

20 Joseph Thomson was the son of James and Mary Thomson and born in Standish 22nd March 1596/7. He matriculated at Queen's College Cambridge in 1622 and took his B.A. degree 1625–6. Despite being a presbyterian replacement for Rev Edward Morton who was expelled, the two seemed to have got on as Thomson does not disappear when he was ejected.

21 Rev Dr G. Wall, S. HELEN'S CHURCH, SEPHTON, Paper read 7th March, 1895.

22 Other early references to pottery in Liverpool include a Robert Lyon listed as a 'Clay potter' in 1643, a delftware mug inscribed 'John Williamson' and dated '1645' and a town order in 1663 that mugs should not be carted through the town.

23 William Chaffers, *Marks and Monograms On Pottery and Porcelain*, p. 286, (London, J. Davy & Sons, 137, Long Acre, 1863).

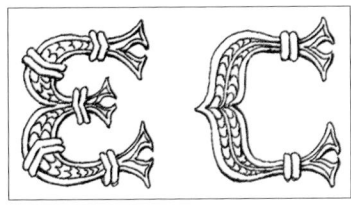

SUBSCRIBERS

Michael James Allen
Canon George Almond
Margaret A. Ashton
Graham K. Austin
Samuel and Sian Austin
Jean Barnes
Paul David Blakey
Beryl Bradbury
Helena Bradbury
Kathleen Braithwaite
Mrs Margaret Brereton
Judith Bristow
The Reverend Steven Brookes
Betty Molyneux Brown
Geoff and Jean Burden
Sakina Burgess
Mary Caroe
Mrs Dorothy Elizabeth Cassapi
John J. Caulfield
Keith Caulkin
Alan E. Chapman
Darren Charnock
David and Pauline Clarkson
John Conway
Katherine and Nicholas Cooper
Peter G. Corbett
Raymond and Carolynne Cotton
Ian Cowell
Paul and Judith Crighton
Peter N. Crighton
Luke A. Crighton
Aileen Cross
Juan Cuervo Forcelledo
H. H. Judith Daley
Peter and Jane Dalton
The Rev'd L. Martin Daniels
Anthony G. Davies
The Rev'd Nicholas E. Davis
Mr Christopher and Mrs Diana Davis
Joanne and Allan Diamond
Netta Dixon

Michelle Dooley
S. J. Duckworth
Philip Duffy
Mary Eccles
Valerie Eckstein
Anthony Edington
Catherine Emley
Jean Entwistle
Anne Lorraine Faichney
Dorothy Joan Faichney
Frank William Farr
George and Eunice Fitzhenry
William Gardner
William and Elizabeth Gibson
William J. Gilpin
Bill Glennon
Jan Grace
Nick Haddow
Ivie Haigh
Philip M. Halewood
Carl Hampson
Adrian Hanks
David Hanks
Peter and Jean Healey
Tom and Geraldine Hickson
Peter W. Howe
Mrs Jean Hughes
Andrew Instone-Cowie
Joyce E. Jenkins
Pat Johnson
Murielle Jones
Lady Kay
Peter Kennerley
Dr Trevor Kirkham
James William Knell
Anne Lanceley
Maureen Lavelle
Barry and Judith Leonard
Sheila Llewellyn
Sheila MacKenzie
Lynn MacKinnon

Christina Mallinson
Henry Marsden
Paul K. Martin
Bryan J. McCahey
The Rev'd Nicola Milford
Norma and Brian Milligan
Claire and Lenard Mitchell
Javier Monforte Munoz
Patricia Moore
Mrs Wendy D Moores
John S. Moseley
Stephen Richard Moss
Stuart and Suzanne Newton
Nightingale Tony
Ormskirk and District
    Family History Society
Doreen Owens
Andrew Pearce
Bill Pickup
Margaret A. Pinder
Ian and Rowena Preston
David Price
June and Ian Ray
Joy Rigby
William John Roberts
Lyn Royan
Angela Rushton
Andrew and Kathy Rushton

Neil Shacklady
Karen Smith
Elizabeth Alice Smith
John Sparkhall
Craig W. A. Staples
W. L. Steadman
Floris Stoter
Brian Sutcliffe
Catherine Tattershall
Helen P. Taylor
Graham and Elizabeth Turner
Aidan Turner-Bishop
Ann Walters
Margaret Walton
Philip and Anne Watmough
Bryan Webb
Chris Webster
Hazel and Graham White
Brian Whitlock Blundell
Nicholas C. Willasey
Betty Williams
Philip and Elizabeth Wilson
Mr John and Mrs Penelope Woodhead
Mr David and Dr Becky Woodhead
Ray and Lucy Woods
Arthur and Pam Wright
Mrs Patricia Wright
John Dale Zacharias

ACKNOWLEDGEMENTS

Hindsight is a wonderful thing but I fear that it would kill off many noble endeavours. To provide a guide to a church and parish like Sefton has been a fascinating but perilous journey.

I have received widespread support on this quest. First I must mention Mark Blundell of Crosby, James Weld of Lulworth Estate and Christopher Rainshaw Rothwell of Lulworth. These three gentlemen have provided invaluable insights and information about their respective families and in Mark's case permission to use the *Diary of Nicholas Blundell* and important rarely seen pictures. The Dean of the Metropolitan Cathedral and Dean Emeritus Mgr Peter Cookson kindly allowed access to historic Molyneux silverware held in the Treasury. I must also thank Mary Caroe for her kindness, hospitality and help.

From the *Friends of Sefton* I am indebted to Sybil and Keith Thomas for their encouragement, H. H. Judith Daley for her contribution about the Worthies' Window, Helen Hunter for her assessment of the great East Window, Craig W. A. Staples for his useful photographs, Margaret Walton and John Slater. I am also particularly grateful to John Quirk who spent many hours checking facts and making valuable suggestions.

A number of people have kindly lent material, such as Dilly Hayman, Tony and Eileen Edington, Arthur and Pam Wright, and Irene McKay who generously provided photographs taken by her late husband, Allan Lee.

At the proof stage I am grateful to Mark Blundell who meticulously surveyed the material, corrected historical errors and suggested useful amendments. Rev'd Nicholas Davis visited Sefton and tested the Guide, and nothing escaped his notice. Helena Bradbury kindly scrutinised the text and was meticulous in her attention to detail.

Andrew Mather and Christine Beatty of AMA DataSet Limited Preston with Robin Utracik of Northern Studios have been the driving force behind the attractive design and layout of the book. Many of Robin's photographs bring the book to life and Andrew has five generations of family experience behind him in printing and book production . . . and it shows in the appearance of this book.

The Rector and Church Wardens have given me total access to the church and related material and this has helped me enormously. Mark Blundell has kindly provided an uplifting *Foreword* to *The Cathedral of the Fields* and Rev Nicola Milford an inspiring *Introduction* to the stand-alone *Guide Book*.

Finally and most importantly, I am extremely grateful to the Sponsors for their generosity and confidence and the large number of Subscribers who have supported this project.

Like all historical books, this too will be found wanting, but I hope that you will discover many positive and attractive aspects which will outweigh any peccadilloes.

Edmund James Crighton
September 2016

SELECT BIBLIOGRAPHY

Margaret Blundell, *A Lancashire Squire*, (Oxfordshire, Day Books and Mark Blundell, 2002).

Richard Brooke, *Liverpool as it Was, 1775 to 1800*, (London, J. Mawdsley and Son, 1853).

W. D. Caröe, Sefton, *A Descriptive and Historical Account*, (London, Longmans, Green and Co., 1893).

Charles T. Gatty, F.S.A., *The Liverpool Potteries*, (Paper read before the Historic Society of Lancashire and Cheshire, 24th March, 1881).

Matthew Gregson, *Portfolio of Fragments*, (London, George Routledge and Sons, 1869).

Rev. Thomas Elison Gibson, *Lydiate Hall and its Associations*, (Southport, Valentine, Hanson and Co., 1876).

Rev. J. P. Hobson, M.A., *Sephton Church*, (Liverpool, Littlebury Bros. Ltd., 1935).

Rev. E. Horley, M.A., The *Mock Corporation of Sephton*, (Paper read before the Historic Society of Lancashire and Cheshire, 10th. February, 1881).

Rev. Thomas Elison Gibson, *A Cavalier's Note Book*, (London, Longmans, Green and Co., 1880).

Frank Tyrer, *The Blundell Family of Crosby*, (Sefton Libraries and Arts Services, 1990).

Frank Tyrer, *The Great Diurnal of Nicholas Blundell of Little Crosby, Lancashire*, (Record Society of Lancashire and Cheshire, 1972).

Rev. G. W. Wall, *St Helen's Church, Sephton*, (Paper read before the Historic Society of Lancashire and Cheshire, 7th. March, 1895).